THE VERTICAL WORLD
OF YOSEMITE

THE

A COLLECTION OF PHOTOGRAPHS

VERTICAL WORLD OF YOSEMITE

AND WRITINGS ON ROCK CLIMBING IN YOSEMITE

EDITED BY GALEN A. ROWELL

WILDERNESS PRESS, BERKELEY, CALIFORNIA

**Wilderness Press
2440 Bancroft Way
Berkeley, CA 94704**

*Library of Congress Card Catalog Number: 73–85908
ISBN: 911824-28-6 (cloth edition)
ISBN: 911824-87-1 (paper edition)
Designed by Dave Comstock*

Printed in Japan

The following articles are reprinted by the kind permission of their publishers and authors.

"An Ascent of Half Dome in 1884," *Sierra Club Bulletin,* 1946

"The First Ascent of the Higher Cathedral Spire," *Sierra Club Bulletin,* 1934

"Five Days and Nights on the Lost Arrow," *Sierra Club Bulletin,* 1948

"Ordeal by Piton," *Sierra Club Bulletin,* 1951

"The Northwest Face of Half Dome," *Sierra Club Bulletin,* 1958.

"El Capitan," *American Alpine Journal,* 1959

"Realm of the Overhang," *Sierra Club Bulletin,* 1962

"The Salathe Wall, El Capitan," *American Alpine Journal,* 1963

"Modern Yosemite Climbing," *American Alpine Journal,* 1963

"Camp Four," *Mountain,* July 1969

"The South Face of Mount Watkins," *American Alpine Journal,* 1965

"The North America Wall," *American Alpine Journal,* 1965

"Muir Wall—El Capitan," *American Alpine Journal,* 1966

"Rescue on the South Face of Half Dome," *Summit,* May 1969

"Tis-sa-ack," *Ascent,* 1970

"Reflections of a Broken-down Climber," *Ascent,* 1971

"*Mountain* Interview: Royal Robbins," *Mountain 18,* November 1971

■ I meant to tell mankind to aspire to a new state about which I could tell them little or nothing, to teach them to tread a long and lonely path which might or might not lead thither, to bid them dare to encounter all possible perils of nature unknown, to abandon all their settled manners of living and to cut themselves off from their past and their environment, and to attempt a quixotic adventure with no resources beyond their native strength and sagacity. I had done it myself and found not only that the pearl of great price was worth far more than I possessed, but that the very perils and privations of the quest were themselves my dearest memories. I was certain of this at least: that nothing in the world except this was worth doing.

Aleister Crowley

CONTENTS

INTRODUCTION

■ WHAT is enticing about struggling up a granite wall in the California heat? Why would men give up the pleasantries of 20th century living to exert themselves and sometimes suffer with no tangible reward in sight? What motivates those who climb and what goes on in their heads?

■ Hopefully the reader will no longer ask these questions after finishing this book. It is not a history of Yosemite climbing, for that would entail making judgments of someone else's experiences. Instead it is a series of glimpses into the traditions of technical climbing written by the participants themselves. Unlike in other sports, the great majority of mountain writings and photographs come from the participants, not from trained observers. It could be said that this collection of narratives effectuates a history, but it does not. The writers themselves have narrowed the choice of topics and events. As an example, we print Charles Pratt's story of the south face of Mt. Watkins, a hauntingly lyrical account of a big-wall climb in the middle Sixties. Historically, Pratt's ascent of the Crack of Doom in 1961, a route that remained for years the hardest free climb in Yosemite, was more important. But since Pratt chose not to write about the Crack of Doom, its first ascent will remain only a page in the guidebook and a legend told around a campfire.

■ These accounts of adventure go far in answering indirectly most questions about technique, equipment and personal relationships. Since they are about single events, usually the ascent of a new climb, they are shy on general information about how, why and where Yosemite climbing began. Let's examine some frequently asked questions before we begin reading accounts written during eras that we may not understand.

■ What are the roots of technical climbing in Yosemite? Where and when did it begin? Many climbers say it started with the ascent of the Cathedral Spires in 1934. Others point to the ascent of Lunch Ledge, part way up Washington Column, in September 1933. But the roots go much deeper than the first successes with rope and piton.

■ The question of the first technical climb may be more a problem of semantics than of facts. Ropes and eye bolts were used on the first ascent of Half Dome in 1875. The only thing separating that ascent from the more modern type of climbing was the lack of a running belay—a rope fed to the leader by a stationary second man.

■ The *Climber's Guide to the High Sierra* reports that Francis Farquhar and Robert Underhill introduced the proper use of the rope to the Sierra Nevada on the north face of Unicorn Peak in 1931. A recent interview with Farquhar, now in his eighties, cast new light on the information that survived three editions of the guidebook. Robert Underhill was on the East coast at the time of the Unicorn ascent. In the summer of 1930 he taught Farquhar rope management, which he had learned in Europe, during a Harvard Mountaineering Club outing in the Selkirk Range of British Columbia. Farquhar was then editor of the *Sierra Club Bulletin* and he invited Underhill to write an article about roped climbing. He also invited Underhill to join the Sierra Club's 1931 annual outing for several weeks. The Unicorn climb was made before the outing and was the first of many that summer. After Underhill joined the group, roped climbs were made on Temple Crag and Thunderbolt Peak in the Palisades, and a grand finale on the east face of Mt. Whitney. The 2,000-foot climb was made in just over three hours, a much faster time than most ascents today, when the route is known, equipment is improved and technique is developed far beyond the expectations of the Thirties.

■ Underhill's article, "On The Use And Management Of The Rope In Rock Work", is prominent in the 1931 *Sierra Club Bulletin*. Today's climbers look at the illustrations with sweaty palms. One series of photographs, showing the body belay, pictures a climber with the rope running over his shoulder, without any anchor, standing at the brink of a cliff. The real surprise is hidden in the "Mountaineering Notes" in the back of the same bulletin. On September 7, 1930 John Mendenhall and Max Van Patten climbed the northeast face of Laurel Mountain. Mendenhall writes, "My companion and I were roped, moved one at a time, and employed the belays." One wonders how many other Laurel Mountains are tucked away in the unwritten history of early Sierra climbing.

■ Unicorn Peak and Laurel Mountain are both climbs that were made without the use of pitons or other rock anchors. They are no more difficult than the summit block of Unicorn's neighbor, Cathedral Peak, which was ascended alone, without a rope, by John Muir in 1869. There is a modern trend among climbers to attempt some of the harder routes of the past with no rope or hardware. If this trend is to be recognized as a valid expression of technical climbing, then John Muir, soloing a route on which ropes are still used by many people today, must be viewed as a pioneer technical climber.

■ Muir pioneered many things. He was the first to actively voice the glacial theory of Yosemite's origin. He was the first conservation lobbyist. He was the founder of the Sierra Club. For years the Club was intimately connected with the development of mountaineering throughout the world. Today its minimal involvement is out of the mainstream of major events in the climbing world. The Club has left the final facets of mountain exploration to concentrate on the politics of conservation, another activity that Muir began. In the minds of many young climbers, the relationship between technical climbing and eco-politics is quite oblique. But there is a direct connection. It is a subtle thread which has affected the destiny of the Sierra Club from the beginning.

■ Is it coincidence that the outstanding conservationists, men like John Muir and David Brower, were also outstanding climbers of their day? Is it also coincidence that neither Muir nor Brower nor Adams nor Farquhar was studying, writing or photographing as part of a pre-planned project for an educational institution? Mountains tend to breed thought undisciplined by normal education or urban life. A British climber who later became a mystic devised a mind exercise for his students in the occult. It consisted of purposely forcing out of one's mind one's favorite two themes of thought for a period of weeks. For one person the two themes might be his family and the soap business. For another it might be old age and the stock market. After ridding the mind of its usual and well-worn avenues of thought, a person acquires a new perspective and realizes the role that tradition and repetition play in his thinking.

■ The new perspective is something that comes naturally from intense mountain activity. The rules of civilized society have little effect on a man crossing an exposed traverse. A scowl or a smile, a soothing tone or a swear word, will not decide the outcome. What counts is his knowledge of the limits of his own ability.

■ Security is the antithesis of a moment of crisis in the mountains, and yet during such moments life seems inestimably precious. "Life itself is a steady state of enormous general improbability," wrote Konrad Lorenz, trying to explain the narrow adaptedness of each species to its environment. The climber adapts his physical and mental behavior to a harsh, tilted world. Environmental adaptations, the very things that define civilized life, are considered in poor style. The climber is forced to return his thinking to the way of the rest of the animal kingdom: instead of changing his surroundings to fit his immediate needs, he must adapt himself to his surroundings. It is easy to see how modern conservation thought came from the chrysalis of the mountain years of its leaders.

■ The idea of adapting oneself is foreign to the modern, scientific, logical mind; it is all too easy to adapt equipment to do the job. But mountaineering is a discipline between man and his technical creations. Only a few classic tools are used, tools that leave behind the same natural environment for succeeding parties. Debates over equipment usually are traceable to items that disturb the natural scene, such as expansion bolts and repeated placing of pitons in the same crack. With enough technology, man can ascend any face of any mountain. There is a railroad tunnel going through the north face of the Eiger in Europe, but no one calls the traverse of the mountain in that fashion "mountaineering." The future of climbing will be in small, self-contained parties making climbs that were previously overcome with fixed ropes and large expeditions.

■ Earlier we mentioned the 1931 Sierra Club annual outing, during which technical climbing began to flower for the first time in California. The outing was chronicled in the next *Sierra Club Bulletin* by a young man named Ansel Easton Adams, who was also engaged in a discipline between man and his technical creations: photography. He immediately foresaw problems in the future philosophy of rock climbing, and he wrote the following words:

   "Rock-climbing, as such, should be accepted with the greatest enthusiasm; yet I feel that certain values should be preserved in our contact with the mountains. While it is rarely a case of the complete ascendancy of acrobatics over esthetics, we should bear in mind that the mountains are more to us than a mere proving-ground of strength and alert skill."

■ Today an increasing number of young people are realizing the implications of overadapting the alpine environment by human force. They realize that the personal rewards of the mountains lie in slipping through Nature's defenses, not in applying a scorched-earth policy by altering the land in order to win it. Reaction against excessive use of expansion bolts and other permanent rock anchors in drilled holes has been blunt. Reinhold Messner calls it, "carrying your courage in your rucksack." Many of the techniques described in the stories in this book are now frowned upon by modern Yosemite climbers. This does not mean that they were wrong at the time, any more than Henry Ford was wrong to make a Model T without a smog device. It does mean that today's climber has to consider the cumulative effects of his actions in a sport that is becoming increasingly popular. Unlike most other sports, the setting is a nonrenewable resource.

■ Why Yosemite? Why have most of the recent developments in technique and equipment been here instead of in the Alps or the Rockies? Were Yosemite climbers more capable and smarter? Or were there special circumstances there acting as catalysts to the ventures of normal men?

■ The Sierra Club climbers of the Thirties soon discovered that Yosemite was a pleasant place to climb. The weather was usually good. Climbs were easily accessible. Physical effort was less at 4,000 feet than in the higher mountains. Friends, dogs, wives and restaurants awaited their return to the Valley floor. Climbing was a moderate exercise. Although practice routes were made on small boulders that were as difficult as many of the hardest parts of today's climbs, the potential of Yosemite as the ideal locale for testing human limits on rock lay dormant. Men in other areas of the world had spent many days and nights in the harsh environment of high mountains—in Alaska and the Himalayas—but in Yosemite, climbing was limited to one-day outings. One factor that limited the length of climbs was the piton. The soft-iron types that were imported from Europe were usually left in place, since removing them would distort or destroy them. Most routes on El Capitan and Half Dome require several hundred piton placements. The beginning of multiday rock climbs came when John Salathé, a Swiss blacksmith, introduced pitons that he forged from the steel of old Ford axles. Since his hard-steel pitons could be hammered back and forth for removal by the last man, a climb requiring hundreds of placements was now possible with a selection of only twenty or thirty pitons.

■ In the postwar years Salathé pioneered several long climbs. Among them were the southwest face of Half Dome, the Lost Arrow from the base, and the north wall of Sentinel Rock. Many of his hardest climbs were made when he was past the age of fifty. They were always accomplished with a minimum amount of food, water, equipment and publicity. His name is still little known beyond the circle of climbers who have gained strength and inspiration from his bold, yet humble, achievements.

■ Many solutions to problems have hidden negative feedback that may not show up for years. Although Salathé introduced hard-steel pitons a quarter century ago, it is only quite recently that they have been derided because of crack damage from their constant placement and removal. Today's climbers in Yosemite use artificial chocks—jam nuts—as much as possible on the popular routes. Rock climbing has come almost full circle. Fixed pitons and sometimes bolts are being advocated to avoid further crack damage. Yesterday's vertical wilderness is in danger of becoming a worn granite pegboard in a well-used outdoor gymnasium.

■ Climbing is like the four-minute mile: once a barrier is surmounted, the impossible is oft-repeated. Yesterday's incredible feats are today's old classics. A decade ago America's best climbers stood in awe of El Capitan, and few considered personally attempting it. Recently it was climbed by a high-school lad during spring vacation. When he had time left over at the end of the week, he climbed the Prow route on Washington Column.

Introduction

■ However, this book is not about such feats. Its thread of continuity is that each chapter is somehow related to the wonder, awe and mystery of Yosemite's walls when some of them were unclimbed. The creaking door is closing on the Golden Age, the age of discovery and exploration, of Yosemite climbing. There are no grand faces awaiting first ascents by future generations. But as Yvon Chouinard wrote in *Modern Yosemite Climbing* (1963), the future of Yosemite Valley will be as a "training ground for a new generation of super-alpinists who will venture forth to the high mountains of the world to do the most esthetic and difficult walls on the face of the earth."

—Galen A. Rowell

AN ASCENT OF HALF DOME IN 1884

A. PHIMISTER PROCTOR

[*The first visitors to the Valley imagined that Half Dome must once have been a whole dome, one side of which was sheared away in some ancient colossal disaster. An early theory was that the bottom had suddenly dropped out of the Valley, leaving the steep cliffs of El Capitan and Half Dome. Later, John Muir theorized that a glacier had cleanly chopped away the front of the dome. Modern geologists have concluded that the upper part of Half Dome was never glaciated. □ Although man finds it strangely satisfying to explain his surroundings by cataclysmic events, it appears that the dome is the result of slow geological processes that were well on their way before the coming of the ice ages. Natural joints in the rock—and in some places the lack of them—guided the final form. Ice may have been responsible for the present clean appearance and lack of debris at the base of Half Dome's cliffs, but the superb natural architecture of the dome cannot be attributed to any single geological event. □ On three sides the faces of Half Dome are at least 1500 feet high. On the fourth—the northeast—easy scrambling brings one to a shoulder only 700 feet from the summit. Today, a trail leads to the shoulder and an easy though airy cable system goes to the summit. The first ascent of the dome was made on this face in 1875 by George Anderson, who drilled laboriously for weeks in order to anchor a hand line to the top. Phimister Proctor climbed the dome nine years later. Avalanches had torn down most of the ropes and several of the bolts. Proctor wrote this article some sixty years after his climb, at the request of Francis Farquhar, for the 1946 issue of the* Sierra Club Bulletin. *This harrowing tale of curling bare toes around bolts, throwing the lasso and using ropes that were frayed from picketing horses should give pause to modern hikers and climbers who safely scramble up the dome in a few hours.*]—G.A.R.

■ AFTER a good summer and fall of sketching at Grand Lake and Flattop Mountain my horses' heads were, in the autumn of 1883, pointed toward Denver. I had taken a studio on Laramie Street preparatory to a winter's work in engraving and painting, and was about ready to put out my shingle when, to my surprise, Alden Sampson, of New York, with whom I had been on a couple of hunting trips, dropped in. He was anxious for a sketching and hunting trip and invited me to join him. As prospects for making a living in Denver that winter were exceedingly slim, I accepted the invitation with alacrity. It was December, however, and the Rockies were out of the question and Mexico at that time was infested with bandits. We finally decided on California. I looked forward to new scenes for sketching, new experiences, and some hunting. So, with sketching and hunting outfits, we boarded a Santa Fe train for Los Angeles.

■ In those days Los Angeles was a picturesque, semi-Mexican town. Its

1

streets were paved with mud ankle deep. We stayed at a hotel with a patio filled with tropical fruit and flowers. Having just come out of the Rockies with their two or more feet of snow, we found the contrast striking. Where the finest buildings now are, were most of the corrals where we bought our horses. We chose five: Spider, Buck, Pinto, Pink, and Rattlesnake—"Rattler," for short. The last was a snake, for sure.

■ We left Los Angeles as soon as we had assembled our paraphernalia. Our first night out of Los Angeles was spent in Pasadena. I can remember only half a dozen houses in the place then, but, even so, pack horses were quite a novelty, and we created some excitement. We had decided to go up the Wilson Trail until the rainy season was over, and the next afternoon saw our outfit going up the zigzags.

■ After a pleasant stay of a couple of months on the Wilson Trail, we packed into the Mojave desert, hunting antelope and sketching. In six months we traveled 1500 miles through California and wound up in Yosemite.

■ "That's Half Dome," said a voice, "right across the Valley." I was sitting on Overhanging Rock, with my feet hanging over the Yosemite Valley, 3,000 feet below. Turning I saw, standing near by, a man who turned out to be Galen Clark, one of the pioneers of the valley. He told us how, several years before, an intrepid sailor named Anderson had with great labor and danger put up a rope cable on Half Dome. A year or so before our advent, he said, Anderson had died, and during the past winter an avalanche had taken down most of his cable and had torn out many of its supporting pins. "Now," he said, "we are waiting for some Swiss Alpine climbers to come over and replace the rope."

■ At that last remark our ears went forward. The thought passed through both our minds at the same instant: "No foreigner will do that job till we have a try at it."

■ We camped half a mile from Glacier Point for some days, enjoying the wonderful valley views, then moved to Little Yosemite where we established a base for our attempt on Half Dome.

■ A day or so later we were standing at the bottom of the 1500-foot, smooth, granite pitch. The only side it was possible to climb appeared to be as smooth as writing paper. At our feet lay the remains of the bale-rope cable which had been torn down by the snow slide.

■ As we studied the face of the mountain, we saw how the dare-devil sailor had accomplished his work. He had climbed up the steep grade wherever there was the slightest toe-hold; then, when he could go no farther, he reached up as far as he could and drilled a six-inch hole. In this he fastened a bolt one-half inch in diameter which stuck out from the rock about two inches over all. One end of the bolt was bent into a ring through which he fastened his cable. This he had fashioned by stringing a number of bale ropes until the cable was about three inches in diameter. To keep it from tangling, he bound it every foot. When each pin was well secured in the granite, he attached the cable to the pin ring by a smaller rope. Then, standing on that pin he would drill another hole and again attach the cable.

■ Wherever it was possible to climb, and he was a past master at that game, he went without pins, taking advantage of toe-holds. Then, when the rock was too smooth and steep, another pin was put in and the cable

An Ascent of Half Dome in 1884

Proctor's route on the northeast face of Half Dome was close to that of the present cable stairway, visible just left of center.

fastened as he went. This helped him to come and go. He had built a cabin at the nearest spring, a mile away, where he lived and kept his forge for making bolts.

■ We returned to camp that night after our tour of inspection to get ready to tackle the cliff in the morning. We had carried with us all of our pack and picket ropes that could be spared, and both of us were looking forward to the attempt with considerable anxiety.

■ Everything ready, we started on the ascent. The first two hundred feet were accomplished, all the rope hauled up and fastened, and then our troubles began in earnest. We tried every expedient we could think of, one after the other, to get up that smooth steep rock. We could see clearly enough now why all the others had failed, for no matter how hard we tried we kept slipping back. Yet, forty feet or so above our heads a rock jutted out. If we could only reach it! Beyond, the surface looked rough enough for

Proctor, a well known artist and sculptor, drew this sketch of himself on Half Dome from memory more than 60 years after his ascent.

finger-holds for some distance. But there was no joy in that, for we couldn't get there. We had failed! There was one satisfaction—no one would know of our failure, for we had told no one of our intentions. In silence we began to gather up our ropes.

■ Suddenly I had an inspiration. "I'll lasso it," I yelled. No one had thought of that—the only possible solution, except for Anderson's laborious method. Luckily I was a pretty fair hand with a lariat. Tying a loop on a lash rope, I made a throw. After several false pitches I finally got the range. The knot caught in a crack of the rock and stuck. It didn't look particularly good to me, but I started crawling up the steep slope supporting my weight on the rope. Just before I could grasp the projection, the knot slipped and down I slid for about twenty feet before it caught again. This gave me a bad scare, and while I was collecting my scattered nerves, Sampson climbed up. Soon we were both standing on the jutting rock and could survey the problem ahead.

■ We found that the slide had not only carried away all of the rope and some of the pins but had loosened some of the pins that were left. This was an unlooked for handicap. Wherever a pin had been pulled out, the only way to reach the next one was to lasso it and then pull oneself up to it with the help of the rope.

4

An Ascent of Half Dome in 1884

■ As we proceeded we found that some of the pins had been bent over by the snow and were difficult to rope. Often my loop would roll over a ring twenty times before I caught, even though I had made a good throw. Several of the pins pulled out when my weight was put on the rope. Moreover, our ropes had been used in packing and picketing horses for the past six months and were rather thin and frayed. By this time I was barefoot, for I had discarded my shoes which had a poor set of hobnails.

■ When I reached a pin, my method was to climb up on it, always leaning against the wall of the mountain, and hook my big toe over the pin. That was my only support. I would straighten myself up slowly, still leaning against the face of the mountain, and throw for the next pin. And I repeat, I was standing on a two-inch pin, with my big toe the only support between me and the valley below. There was never a handhold. The only way that I could get my big toe over the ring was to double up like a jackknife, put my toe on the fingers by which I was holding to the pin, and when I was balanced all doubled up, pull my fingers out with all my weight still resting on them. This was not too easy, as I soon found out. Early in the day my right glove got away from me and went tobogganing down the mountain. This made changing my weight from fingers to toe much more painful.

■ We at length reached a place where there were no pins, but there were a few rough surfaces. It was now Sampson's turn to go ahead. I doled out the belt rope as he cautiously crawled aloft. If he had slid down past me there wasn't a chance in the world that I could stop him, and we would both have been swept to the bottom. Finally, he reached a ledge where he was compelled to slant off to the side, and this was impossible without something to hold to. As he hung on desperately to small cracks in the rock, he worked a piece of bale-rope from his pocket and tied it to a small bush just above him. I held my breath. Then, putting just enough pressure on the rope to keep himself from slipping, he moved cautiously along till the angle was too great and he had to let go of the rope. But he managed to drag himself to a little hump in the rocks, where he cupped his hand over it and clung for several minutes to get his breath. Several yards farther he reached a safe spot, where he fastened the rope and I pulled up to him.

■ By noon we had reached the only ledge on the mountainside where we could rest and eat lunch. It was all of six inches wide and had been forced away from the main rock so that we could push a leg down in it and rest without holding on. I tell you, that felt good.

■ By the end of the first day we had made about half of the distance. Just before sunset we slid down the cable, mounted our horses and rode to camp some three miles away. My feet were mighty sore from climbing about on the rocks. To tell the truth, I looked at that mountain with a heap of dread, though I didn't let on. Later I found out that Sampson was scared, too, but as I didn't show any signs of fear, neither would he.

■ Bright and early the next morning we were back at the starting place with all the rope we possessed. It wasn't hard to reach the upper end of the cable, but there our troubles began. It was tedious work pulling all the spare rope after us. I don't know the exact pitch of the mountain, but everything slipped off the moment we let go of it. Every minute we had to lean against the mountain, which always seemed trying to push us away.

■ From then on, the surface was the deadly smoothness that I

5

Modern tourists climb the cable route pictured on page 3.

dreaded—there were few pins, and I had to go ahead with the lasso. About a hundred and fifty feet above the spot where I took the lead, I was clinging by my big toe to a pin and lying on my side against the steep cliff, trying to rope the next pin. There was a wind blowing, and this made roping difficult. Finally the rope caught. I put my weight on it, and it held. Then just as I was about to let go on my toe-hold I gave another yank and out came the pin! It rolled down past me, still in my lasso loop. That gave me a chill, and no mistake.

■ Luckily the next pin was only five feet above the one I had just pulled out. But the tedious work had to be done all over again. After half an hour of trying, the loop finally caught on that pin. It was a great relief, for if the little pin I was then on had given way, or if my knee had caved in, it would have been all over, for there was nothing between me and the bottom of the canyon.

■ The next pin was the worst of all, for it was thirty-five feet above me on a ledge of rock which stuck out over me about two feet and a half. It seemed next to impossible to make the rope fly up those extra perpendicular feet and hold. We both yelled when the loop finally settled over it. Right there was the fiercest spot I had to conquer. I crawled up on hands and knees, holding like grim death to the rope, until I got to the ledge. There I had to pull myself up on the rope hand-over-hand until I got hold of the pin with my fingers. Then I had to worm myself up over the pin in the "jack-knife" movement while I held my weight on the pin with three fingers of my right hand. With my right big toe over my fingers, I slid my body up against the face of the mountain, first painfully yanking my fingers out from

6

under my toe with all my weight on said toe! I lost some skin, but that couldn't be helped. As I stood leaning against the sloping granite catching my breath, that hellish old mountain seemed more than ever determined to push me off.

■ Once my right toe was hooked over the little pin, there it had to stay. I couldn't change my position, for there was absolutely nothing above to cling to. But before I could catch the next pin, which was a long throw above, my leg trembled so that I simply had to go down—and that was even more difficult than going up! I had to push my index finger under my toe to get hold of the pin, meanwhile hanging over that empty mile of space. It seemed almost impossible to keep from pitching headlong into the blue. I had to climb up over that hellish corner three separate times before I succeeded in roping that next pin. Every time, under the intense strain, my leg would begin to quiver, and I knew that I would either have to go down or get a cramp and fall down. How I cursed the day that I undertook such a fool stunt.

■ At last, after an hour and twenty-five minutes of unbroken hades, my loop held. This pin still had a bunch of old rope caught around it, which made roping it difficult. Four times it caught, but when my weight was put on it the loop had slipped off. I was anything but happy as I put my weight on that worn rope and, on hands and knees, cautiously climbed up the polished surface of the rock. How anxiously I watched the rope for signs of giving way and the loop for signs of slipping off the pin. If either had happened, you wouldn't be reading this story. To the left, through the corner of my eye, I could see Little Yosemite 3,000 feet below, while at the right, bathed in purple mist, lay the grand Yosemite Valley. Below me, clinging to the face of the cliff, Sampson looked little bigger than a chipmunk. Curiously, while lying there against the side of the mountain I thought to myself, "Now I can face the biggest grizzly in the wilds."

■ Finally I reached a safe pin, and to it fastened the rope. Sampson climbed up then, and we pulled the cable after us. From here up we had to use about two hundred feet of our own rope to piece out the sailor's cable. There just wasn't enough to finish the job. Sampson still had some ticklish work to do, but we made the top at last.

■ The view from the top of Half Dome is, I suppose, one of the most wonderful in all America. The valley was spread out below us in all its blue, hazy beauty. We sat for awhile enjoying the wonders of the valley under the glow of the setting sun, and then built a fire on the highest point in view of the whole valley, to let people know that Half Dome had been conquered! At last, reluctantly, we left, slid down the cable and reached safety just at dark.

■ There are times in a young man's life that a great experience changes it. Those two days on Half Dome were for me the divide between careless youth and serious manhood. My mind had been made up long ago to become an artist. There was nothing else for me in the way of a profession. Those hours of anxiety and danger, trying to accomplish something which in itself was of little value to the world, had crystalized in my mind the ideals that had vaguely been floating in it. After a month's visit in San Francisco with an artist friend, I returned to Denver and was soon launched upon the career that has claimed me ever since.

THE FIRST ASCENT OF THE HIGHER CATHEDRAL SPIRE

BESTOR ROBINSON

[*Why are climbers attracted to spires? Psychologists come up with astonishing reasons. While not discounting the possibility of phallic worship, I feel the answer is even more simple. A spire is the ultimate summit. It need not be shared with anyone who did not come up the hard way. A face climb may be harder or longer, but its summit is usually accessible by an easier route. □ In the early 1930's, when pitons and the running belay were introduced to Yosemite, the tops of a few spires were the only unclimbed summits. One spire, Split Pinnacle, was mysteriously ascended on a ramshackle ladder by an unknown party—a far more dangerous climb than modern ascents with nylon ropes and piton anchors. This ascent was made possible by the fact that unroped scrambling leads to a position only thirty feet from its summit. Another spire, the Lost Arrow, was to wait until after the war. Its first ascent was by means of a rope thrown from the rim of the Valley. But the Cathedral Spires were long climbs, well separated from any other cliffs. By logic we would assume that the ascents of these towers would come after many of the easier routes in the Valley had been climbed. Yet the ascent of the Higher Spire, on April 15, 1934, was one of the first technical rock climbs in Yosemite. On August 25 of the same year, the same party climbed the Lower Spire. These ascents mark the beginning of modern rock climbing in Yosemite. Bestor Robinson's account first appeared in the 1934* Sierra Club Bulletin.]*—G.A.R.*

■ ALL of the peaks in and near Yosemite Valley, with but two exceptions, were climbed in the eighteen-seventies. It was but natural that Yosemite should have attracted early mountain climbers, for even in those days its scenic grandeur was well publicized, and, compared to other Sierra Nevada regions, it was readily accessible. The two Cathedral Spires, however, remained unscaled.

■ In the intervening half-century the native ability of our rock-climbers has probably not improved. Climbing technique and climbing equipment, on the other hand, have been developed remarkably in the last few years. The seed of the lore of pitons, carabiners, rope-downs, belays, rope traverses, and two-man stands was sown in California in 1931 by Robert L. M. Underhill, a member of the Appalachian Mountain Club, with considerable experience in the Alps. That seed has sprouted and grown in California climate with exuberant vigor sufficient to satisfy the most vociferous Chamber of Commerce.

■ So it was not strange that three of the devotees of this new technique of

9

Lower Cathedral Spire looms in the background as a modern climber nears the summit of Higher Cathedral Spire.

climbing, two of them members of Underhill's original Sierra party, should be found reconnoitering the Cathedral Spires for two days in the summer of 1933, looking for a possible route of ascent of the higher spire.

■ That reconnoitering trip, and subsequent examination of photographs under microscope and protractor, made it evident that the ascent of the higher spire would involve far more difficult climbing than anything that had been previously attempted by any member of the party. The average slope of the four faces of this spire was found to be 81°. The utter absence of cracks and the existence of massive overhangs on some of the gentler (75°-80°) slopes made it clear that several traverses would be necessary on the steepest side.

■ So, in November, 1933, reinforced by what seemed an ample supply of freshly imported pitons and carabiners, we started our climb. Darkness turned us back at "second base" with our piton supply practically exhausted.

■ A new supply of pitons arrived during the winter. On April 15, 1934, we made the ascent. Climbing were Richard M. Leonard, Jules M. Eichorn, and myself. Watching at the base, photographing and cheering, were Marjory Bridge, Helen Le Conte, Doris Corcoran, Francis P. Farquhar (the club's president), and Bert Harwell, Chief Naturalist of Yosemite National Park.

■ We spent two hours clambering over talus-slopes from the floor of the valley up to the wash lying to the west of the higher spire to the point where the talus gives way to the cliffs that form the south rim of Yosemite Valley. Here the watching party settled for a day of leisure, while the climbing party started upward with the following equipment: Two half-inch ropes (120 feet long, tensile strength 2650 pounds); 200 feet of roping-down line (tensile strength 1000 pounds); 60 feet of extra rope, for slings; 55 pitons, assorted; 13 carabiners; two piton-hammers, with slings attached; three piton step-slings; extra clothing; first-aid kit; two small cameras; one motion-picture camera; and lunch.

■ From the talus to the southwest of the spire a long crack opening into a chimney gives easy access to a broad ledge, which on our attempt of the previous November we had dubbed "First Base." From this point our route lay directly up and over an overhang, then by rope traverse around the southwest nose of the spire onto the perpendicular west face. We remembered the remarkable sense of balance and ability to stick to next to nothing that Eichorn had shown when on the previous November he had surmounted the overhang and fixed two pitons on the very nose of the traverse. The eleven pitons we had used at this stage we found to be as firm as when we had left them six months before. The traverse ended at a steep crack, excellent in its climbing possibilities, but dizzily overhanging hundreds of feet of empty space. Without the necessity of pitons and with occasional scrub oaks as anchorages we made good time up this crack to "Second Base," the lofty ledge which marked the end of our previous attempted ascent, and on this occasion marked time out for lunch.

■ There is a real thrill in munching an orange while perched on a one-foot ledge, roped to the mountain for safety, and watching orange-peels drop perpendicularly to the talus below without once touching the mountainside.

■ Lunch over, we were faced with the most difficult stretch of the entire climb—a long chimney too wide for bracing and, worst of all, ending in an overhanging wall devoid of cracks suitable for pitons. But the lower part of the chimney took pitons well. One by one they were placed by Eichorn and Leonard, as they alternated at this exhausting work, while I tended the two ropes which we were here using to insure absolute safety. A clever rope-traverse out of the chimney to the north by Leonard, a two-man stand, and we were up. Thirty feet of climbing had taken fifteen pitons and two and one-quarter hours.

■ The rock was now more broken, and climbing was easier. It seemed more and more certain that success would shortly be ours as we moved steadily up a series of connected cracks which led to a high wide ledge just under the summit on the west face of the peak. The summit block, however, was sheer, without any convenient one-eighth-inch cracks designed for receiving pitons. How exasperating to be forty feet below the top and no route in sight, especially with the sun setting! Hopefully, we followed this ledge to the south to see what we could see. Since it continued under the overhang of the summit block, it was necessary to crawl, gazing down occasionally while wiggling across gaps where small sections of the ledge had dropped away.

■ On the south face of the peak we found the crack we had been hoping for. It was almost perpendicular, too small for handholds or footholds, but it would take pitons. Twelve pitons we drove into it and used them for the ascent without additional handholds or footholds. Then a ledge, a two-man stand, a little scrambling, and we were on the flat-topped summit.

■ The sun had already set. Hurriedly we built a cairn, raised an American flag on a stumpy improvised flagpole of huckleberry oak, took pictures, and signed the register which we had lugged to the top.

■ The descent was sheer joy. Roping off one-hundred feet at a stretch from ledge to ledge, never having to use tired fingers and toes on handholds or footholds, we had nothing to bother about except the temperature of our pants as the rope converted mechanical energy into heat. In forty-five minutes we descended, in ease, what had taken nearly nine hours of difficult climbing to ascend.

■ Looking back upon the climb, we find our greatest satisfaction in having demonstrated, at least to ourselves, that by the proper application of climbing technique extremely difficult ascents can be made in safety. We had practiced belays and anchorages; we had tested pitons and ropes by direct falls; we had tried together the various maneuvers which we used on the peak, until three rock-scramblers had been coordinated into a team. The result was that there was no time on the entire climb, but that if any member of the party had fallen, his injuries would, at the worst, have been a few scratches and bruises.

The First Ascent of the Higher Cathedral Spire

Near the top of the left skyline a climber can be seen waving his arms. This remarkable photograph was taken with a 4 x 5 view camera during the first ascent of the Higher Cathedral Spire in 1934.

(L to R) Bestor Robinson, Richard Leonard and Jules Eichorn on the summit of Higher Cathedral Spire. Note the American flag and tennis shoes. The photo was made with a self-timer.

The team of Robinson, Leonard and Eichorn wave from the summit of Lower Cathedral Spire, which they ascended for the first time a few months after climbing the Higher.

FIVE DAYS AND NIGHTS ON THE LOST ARROW

ANTON NELSON

[In September 1946, Jack Arnold, Robin Hansen, Fritz Lippmann and Anton Nelson made the first ascent of the Lost Arrow Spire. It must have been a great disappointment for John Salathé, who had made two valiant attempts to climb it. On one of these he rappelled into the notch, 250 feet below the rim, and climbed solo to a stance known today as "Salathé Ledge." This was not easy climbing. Nelson later described it as being "like stepping out the window from the hundredth floor of the Empire State Building onto a window ledge." From the end of the "window ledge", Salathé belayed himself up steep and difficult direct-aid climbing for more than a hundred feet to a little ledge. He retreated and returned the following week with John Thune, climbing to a point only 50 feet below the summit. There were no unsurmountable obstacles. They came down at the end of the day, knowing that the remaining distance could be covered by the same techniques they had been using. □ Before Salathé came back to finish his route, Arnold, Hansen, Lippmann and Nelson forged a plan of their own. Nelson stated the plan as this: "From the brow of the cliff just west of Yosemite Point it is but 100 feet or so laterally to the top of the Arrow, which stands somewhat below the level of the valley rim. If a light line can be cast over the top and down the far side, and then reached by climbing around to it, heavier ropes that would support a man may possibly be pulled over and anchored. Then the last unclimbable pitch can be surmounted by climbing up the rope itself and a unique and spectacular means of returning to the rim can be rigged—an aerial traverse." The incredible plan succeeded and in September 1946 the summit of the Lost Arrow felt its first human footsteps. □ Salathé was not a man to be outdone. What followed a year later was perhaps the boldest single jump in the history of Yosemite climbing. No one had ever spent more than a single night on a Valley climb, but "Ax" Nelson and John Salathé spent five days and nights climbing the Lost Arrow from a point near the base of Upper Yosemite Fall. First they followed a chimney that led for 1,200 feet to the notch beneath the final spire. Then they completed the route on the tip that Salathé and Thune had nearly finished the year before. This was the first "big wall" climb in Yosemite. Anton Nelson's modest account first appeared in the 1948 Sierra Club Bulletin.]—G.A.R.

■ WHAT IS required to climb Yosemite's Lost Arrow? For years many determined men had tried to find out just that. In trying they succeeded only in showing how terribly close to unclimbable the Arrow really is. Then, on September 3, 1947, John Salathé and I completed a successful assault which we had begun 103 hours earlier at the base of the spire.

■ True, men had stood atop its summit one year before when a trip from the rim was ingeniously engineered by four Sierra Club climbers. Spectacular and effective though it was, this maneuver required very little real climbing; it was in effect an admission of the Arrow's unclimbability. The problem the Arrow poses for the climber is to ascend from the base up through the ramparts of the great chimney that cuts the spire away from the cliff, and past the three intermediate ledges, called Errors, until he reaches the summit, facetiously called the Fourth or Last Error.

■ A full story, although it ought to be exciting, would take too much space for present purposes. In its stead, a brief description of the preparations for the ascent is presented for prospective Arrow-climbers:

■ The equipment carried was the best we could make or buy. The only expensive item demanded by this "poor man's sport" was a 120-foot nylon rope, 7/16 inch in diameter, used for belaying, which cost $22.00. Two-rope technique was not used; it would have been too burdensome to carry the extra rope and hardware. Alternatively, when carabiner drag increased the static inertia of the rope to an unwieldy point, the leader would descend from his top three pitons. Taking out the lower ones, he would ascend again, leaving one sound piton perhaps every 20 or 30 feet. A 300-foot rappel rope of 5/16-inch Manila supplemented the nylon on the longer leads. A 150-foot length of ¼-inch sisal reserve rope was used for many things besides hauling up the 30-pound pack. Each of us carried 150 feet of stout fishing line for bringing up extra equipment on complex leads.

■ Each man hung on his belt three multiple-knotted slings. Most of the holds for which one would wish were absent on the massive rock, which averages 80 to 90 degrees for two thirds of the route. Thus, nearly one half of the moves upward demanded some type of direct aid. Now slings may be a little messy—for photographers—but hanging directly on the climbing rope for any length of time is unfeasible. It hurts one's kidneys, cramps one's motions, and leaves one always below his highest piton. On the other hand, standing in a sling, one can rise somewhat above his highest piton, thereby extending his reach a foot or two. Hanging directly on the climbing rope makes one a continuous burden to his belayer, and decreases the safety factor in no small degree since the leader's weight is pulling partly outward on the piton instead of downward only. On the Arrow we often used pitons that were barely adequate to sustain a man's weight, sometimes only a part of his weight. Their use would not have been possible without slings. The second man usually ascended by slings attached by prusik knots to a fixed rope. Direct aid was often used, even on successive stances which on a 100-foot practice climb could be climbed by class-five techniques. Safety depends upon an adequate reserve of strength and we simply had to conserve our strength for the long unknown grind ahead. Stirrups of ⅛-inch duralumin prevented the bruising and cramping of foot muscles that is produced by standing in slings in tennis shoes.

■ About 18 pitons were used, but these we drove in hundreds of places. More pitons would have increased the handicap of weight. They were all hand-forged by Salathé. A few horizontals of 10/20 soft iron were of but little use. Those of 60/80 carbon steel were better, and most useful for driving directly into rotten, crackless granite no other device could overcome. Pitons

16

as good or better were made of 40/60 carbon steel with vanadium in it—the alloy from which Model-A Ford axles are made. Some were forged to wide, short blades with hair-thin tips for use in the tiniest cracks. Then there were angle pitons of 10/20 iron such as were used by the Mountain troops. There ought to be even wider pitons.

■ An improved type expansion bolt—a "Dryvin"—was used. The 1½-inch shield fits a ⅜-inch hole. This is slipped over a hanger about one inch wide and four inches long cut from ⅛-inch iron with holes drilled for the shield and for a carabiner. It is secured by driving in a nail or peg ¼ inch in diameter. Tests have shown that in solid granite or other sound rock it will sustain more than 500 pounds pulling directly outward or over 1000 pounds pulling perpendicular to the axis. The beauty of it is that it takes one-ninth as long to drill in as a ¾-inch bolt and is just as strong in design. The holes are made with a ⅜-inch star drill cut to five inches in length and tempered in oil for maximum hardness. These drills fitted into a heavy handle designed to absorb the shock to the hand. Regular masonry twist drills seem satisfactory, too, but carbaloy drills do not seem to cut well in granite or marble. A spare handle, several drills, and parts for a dozen and a half bolts were carried. A third hammer (one can count on dropping one) was carried, also. The best hammer had a steel shaft continuous with the head and a modified claw cut and forged to permit extraction of the drive-in nails of the bolts.

■ Justification for the use of expansion bolts is not required on such a climb as the Arrow. They are a waste of time, however, as a ladder up just any sheer cliff. They are never a substitute for pitons, and are of doubtful use in poor or rotten rock. Their use is fair, it seems, when one is bridging a holdless, flawless, high-angle face on sound rock to a place where pitons or holds can again be used. They were used in only three places on Lost Arrow. Four or five were used for getting out of a converging, overhanging chimney called "The Alcove" in the massive face one pitch above the ledge about a quarter of the way up. This pitch is the key to entering the Great Chimney, a good safety valve for testing a party's fitness to go higher. Three more were used about two-thirds of the way up, where a 150-foot lead of extreme difficulty took eight hours to overcome. They made possible a 20-foot upward traverse across a smooth 90-degree face. Then perhaps ten bolts were used, to supplement two pitons, in the top 50 feet of the flint-hard and flawless Arrow tip.

■ Twelve carabiners were needed. Some special Arrow equipment was invented, including, among other things, what can best be described as a sky hook. This was actually put into play on a traverse of the summit pitch to provide support from an otherwise useless solution pocket that just had to be used.

■ Weight and bulk of equipment was a limiting factor in personal needs, also. Water was the heaviest material, so the supply was limited to three quarts per person and was carried in a plastic bag. This will last up to five days if one does not sweat too much and can discipline the growing temptation to drink. It must be admitted that friends relieved our self-denial on the fourth day with liquid lowered from the rim to Third Error. A number 2 can of fruit juice was held in reserve for a victory toast at the top. Because of the exertions of the day we wet our mouths a little at dawn, took a sip or two at mid-day, and drank most of our liquid at night. Charles Wilts and

Spencer Austin, who had reached the previous high point on this route, warned that too much liquid is a major drawback. The dozen or more cans of fruit juice they jettisoned made one wonder how they ever had the strength to haul it all up or how they ever got in through some of the narrow places.

■ What small amounts of food we ate were rationed in the same way as the water. We believe that the ideal food is raisins, dates, walnuts or peanuts, and fruit-flavored gelatin candies, and that heavier foods, such as starches or meat, would hardly be digestible under the strains of Arrow climbing. We needed no more than four or five pounds per man for the five days. That we should lose a great deal of weight on the climb was assumed.

■ A small first-aid kit was carried, as well as a rubber-sheathed flashlight. To supplement regular clothing against the chill winds of the bivouac, flannel inner pants, long wool socks, and a wool sweater or *light* parka were worn under our own clothes. However, a small, light zeltsack might be a better expedient. Equipment not in use was rolled inside two burlap sacks to prevent its abrading on the rocks.

■ Our basic idea was that we would climb safely or not at all. We understood that rescue from an accident in the Great Chimney was not to be expected. Bombproof belays were in order and unprotected leads of more than 10 or 15 feet were out of order. When the leader had to take a long chance he did so only when pitons (or bolts) that were sound enough for the anticipated fall were near by and the belayer was on special alert. Then the most that could happen (and not infrequently did happen) was that the leader would take a controlled fall and go right back to work.

■ For climbing on the Arrow, great strength is far less important than patience and endurance. On the first ascent each of us had been on the Arrow four times before and twice we had set out together for at least three days' work. On Memorial Day, 1947, the route became the bed of a waterfall and ended in a precarious rappel. On Fourth of July week end, much was learned during two days and a night on the rock, in which Second Error was attained for the first time. Better equipment was needed. We had thought ourselves in the pink of condition, but after only two days the state of nervous and physical exhaustion dictated retreat and far more rigorous preparation for the next attempt.

■ Several bivouacs on cliff walls, with or without warm clothes, taught us not to expect much rest on a climb. I took a hike the length of the John Muir Trail, practicing making long marches with little or no water. Doing that for four days in one's own home is good enough practice for mastering thirst—for learning, that is, how much thirst is to be safely endured. If one lacks time for long periods in the mountains, running steadily for an hour or so is a good way to build up the heart, lungs, nerves, and muscles for the long endurance at higher altitudes needed by any kind of mountaineering activity. To prevent the onset of cramps one needs brisk calisthenics to train climbing muscles far beyond their normal capacities. On the Arrow, failure to hold oneself to comparable preparations may be sufficient to scuttle a team's most carefully laid plans, and it has done so more than once.

■ For prospective Arrow climbers, it is important to have or acquire experience and competence with things mechanical; a manual acquaintance with forces, materials, and their relationships is a must.

Five Days and Nights on the Lost Arrow

■ This brings one to the matter of practical philosophy. One cannot climb at all unless he has sufficient urge to do so. Danger must be met—indeed, it must be *used*—to an extent beyond that incurred in normal life. That is one reason men climb; for only in response to challenge does a man become his best. Yet any do-or-die endeavors are to be condemned. Life is more precious than victory. In the safest possible climbing on the Arrow there is more than enough stimulus from probable and present danger. To know one's limitations and to keep within them is the essence of good sense. A comparatively weak party, sensitive to its weak points and keeping within their limits, will outlive and outclimb the strongest team which proceeds indiscreetly.

■ One thing is *not* an adequate motive for climbing; that is egotism or pride. Yes, most of us who climb usually play to the crowd, as such an article as this may demonstrate. However, mere self-assertion alone has a low breaking point. To keep going day after day under heart-sickening strenuousness requires a bigger, more powerful faith than in oneself or in any concept of superiority.

■ Conversely, I feel that a man who, through emotional temperament or

On the 25th anniversary of the first ascent of the Lost Arrow, a team of climbers repeated the Tyrolean traverse *by stringing a rope from the tip of the spire to the rim of the valley. Most ascents have been made by climbing the rock near the right skyline, still relying on Salathé's expansion bolts.*

habit, is used to the false stimulus of alcohol has two strikes against him before he undertakes a long climb. The psychological impact of continually new and increasing difficulties while one's physical resources seem to be running down is enough without being fettered by an undisciplined imagination or by emotional crutches. Human limitations are indeed more serious than the natural ones to be faced.

■ A brief description of the first ascent may illustrate some of the foregoing points. In 1937 the 350 feet to First Error took 6 hours; 35 pitons were used for protection. In the 1947 ascent of the Arrow, we passed that point, hauling our 30-pound pack between us, in just three hours, using no more than a dozen pitons. Time was a major limiting factor and all possible haste was made when there was a chance. Nearly half the distance, 650 feet, was beat out the first day in the 13 hours before darkness fell.

■ On the second day increasing problems really began slowing us down. We rope-traversed from the detour going out to Second Error back into the narrowest portion of the chimney where it slashes nearly 100 feet into the heart of the cliff. At midday we arrived at the vertical headwall of the chimney where Wilts and Austin had turned back on their second attempt after two and a half days. From then on the class-6 climbing began in earnest; 350 feet were made the second day, 200 each on the next two, and the last 50 feet on the morning of the fifth day. The first pitch of this sort, 150 feet long, was mostly rotten granite. Salathé led for 8 hours without relief, save for the interruption of darkness. Two pitches above this point, massive, overhanging blocks had to be climbed by the exceedingly wide cracks between them. Often there seemed no evident route at all.

■ After the second day our muscles no longer cramped and we put thirst in its place. Bivouacking on the chockstones with our feet dangling, our backs aching where they were being nudged by granite knobs, and our shoulders tugging at their anchors, we got little sleep. Cold winds barely permitted us to keep warm enough for the rest essential to the digestion of food. The hours until dawn that should permit the greater comfort of climbing were passed largely in talk. Food, sleep, and water can be dispensed with to a degree not appreciated until one is in a position where little can be had.

■ Future Arrow climbers need not worry about varying the route; there is problem enough finding just one route, let alone fretting about alternatives. It should be noted in all fairness that on the first ascent the bolt-removing hammer was lost on the first day, necessitating the ruination of nearly all existing bolts. Extra hangers for the upper reaches were needed. Most of the holes are therefore hopelessly jammed with broken-off bolts. The work will have to be done all over again by the next party. Getting off the climb requires a long rappel down the narrow confines of the chimney. However, we prusiked from the Third Error to the rim on a fixed rope, since friends were on hand to help rig it.

■ Frank Kittredge, then superintendent of Yosemite, asked if the 1947 Labor Day ascent of the Lost Arrow were not "the longest and most difficult high climb on record, presumably on sound rock . . . ." It is merely pointed out that Lost Arrow granite can often be far from sound. The Lost Arrow *can* be climbed again, perhaps in only four days. At any rate its superb challenge is there. To those who made the first vertical traverse of its Four Errors it stands as a symbol of high and unforgettable adventure.

ORDEAL BY PITON

ALLEN STECK

[Sentinel Rock stands like a dark tombstone on the shady side of the Valley. It had an early appeal for climbers, who approached the base of the sheer north wall in the Thirties and Forties. John Salathé and "Ax" Nelson climbed the northeast bowl in 1948. In 1949 Allen Steck was part of a team that attempted the north wall. Steck was in his early twenties, a member of a new generation of climbers, and Salathé was over fifty when the two of them made this memorable climb. They learned that heat can be just as formidable an enemy as cold. On their five-day climb they experienced 105° temperatures and carried a minimum of water and food. Most long Yosemite climbs are now being made in the spring and the fall. □ This route remains one of the great classic climbs of Yosemite. Unlike the majority of big climbs, the north wall can be climbed entirely without direct aid, although most parties still use aid on one section rather than make the long diversion to avoid it. Free climbing is so much faster than aid climbing that by the early Sixties ascents of the wall had been made in one day. Once a party has committed itself to a one-day ascent, then the necessary paraphernalia are much less—no bivouac gear and little food or water. By the early Sixties, Tom Frost and Royal Robbins had climbed the route many times. They decided to see how fast they could climb it, and knowing every inch of the way they were able to forgo use of belays in many places. Their ascent took three hours and fourteen minutes. (Most modern ascents still include a bivouac.) □ When Salathé revisited Yosemite after a long absence, he was told of the fast ascent. With quiet admiration, he turned to Allen Steck and said, "Not our route, Al. They climbed another route." □ This was the last of Salathé's great climbs. He climbed for his own reasons and never sought recognition. One legendary tale concerns a group of young hot-shots arguing about climbing ethics (use of fixed ropes, bolts, etc.). Salathé was silent for quite some time, but he finally said, in his thick accent, "Vy cant ve just climb?" □ "Ordeal by Piton" first appeared in the 1951 Sierra Club Bulletin.*]—G.A.R.*

■ THIS story is not unique in the relatively short history of class-six climbing—there are many two- and three-day ascents listed today in the Swiss, Austrian, and Italian Alps; indeed, directly across from Sentinel Rock, in the Yosemite Valley, is the unmistakable spire of the Lost Arrow, climbed from its base for the first time in September of 1947. This five-day ascent by John Salathé and Ax Nelson was considered the greatest achievement of its kind in the history of tension climbing.

■ The Sentinel climb was of equal rank, perhaps even surpassed it—who can say? John used to tell me, as we waited out the sleepless bivouacs, that he couldn't decide which was "better." "You know, Al," he'd say, looking out across the valley at the Lost Arrow, "it's still a pretty good climb. You and Long ought to climb it next." My answer was a despairing grumble: my next climb was going to be Sentinel Dome in a wheelchair.

21

■ I lay awake many a night in Berkeley wondering what this north wall was like above the buttress; it was almost an obsession with me. This sort of feeling is indeed strange to the hiker or fisherman, yet it is typical of the climber.

■ Many have questioned the quality of this sort of achievement, deploring the use of pitons, tension traverses, and expansion bolts, but the record speaks for itself. This is a technical age and climbers will continue in the future to look for new routes. There is nothing more satisfying than being a pioneer.

■ The lure of the Sentinel Wall goes back to 1936, when Morgan Harris, William Horsfall and Olive Dyer made a reconnaissance on the north face. Rising a full 3,000 feet from the grassy floor of the Yosemite Valley, its sheer north exposure presented a fantastic problem in route finding; true, there was only one possible route (i.e., the Great Chimney), still there was the big question: how to use it? They reached the Tree Ledge, a prominent sandy terrace 1,500 feet above the floor, at the very foot of the north wall proper. Although no records exist, undoubtedly Charles Michael and William Kat, in their explorations of the cliffs, had ascended over easy class-four ledges to this terrace.

■ Several years later Morgan Harris and Dave Brower succeeded in reaching the Tree Ledge, and from the westernmost portion of this ledge they pioneered a route across the west face of Sentinel Rock and up its broken south side. The north wall remained untouched until the early 'forties, and, after several attempts by Robin Hansen, Jack Arnold and Fritz Lippmann, a high point was finally established some 150 feet above the Tree Ledge, to the right of the huge buttress that lies up against the lower portion of the wall. The difficulty was severe, but each attempt added to the knowledge of the route. It seemed of little concern that there was over 1,300 feet of tougher climbing yet to do. That problem would take care of itself eventually.

■ In the fall of 1948, Jim Wilson and Phil Bettler took the initiative and reached a ledge a hundred feet still higher, setting a new record. Then in October 1949, a four-man party—Phil Bettler, Jim Wilson, Bill Long, and I—arrived at the Tree Ledge prepared to make the first bivouac on the face, and was able to climb some 200 feet past the old high point. We passed the night on a loose, tilted chockstone directly beneath the 60-foot, 100-degree "Wilson Overhang." One person could stretch out comfortably, but unfortunately there were four of us. No one was able to sleep but Phil, who had taken one of Jim's backache pills to ease his headache—they were knockout pills, a decided must for any climber's bivouac equipment. Cursing Phil for his contented snoring, the rest of us waited out the night. Morning came and we continued up over the overhang, admirably led by Jim, to a new high point about 450 feet above the Tree Ledge. All eight leads were various degrees of class-six climbing, and over fifty pitons had been necessary.

■ Then came the remarkable ascent over the 1950 Memorial Day week end. Bill Long and Phil Bettler, in a two-day ascent, succeeded in reaching the top of the great 800-foot buttress, and thus the first major problem of the wall was conquered. Above the top of the buttress stretched the final 700-foot face, whose broad expanse was broken only by the Great Chimney, a large

*Bill Long follows a rope traverse during an early attempt to climb
the north wall of Sentinel Rock.*

*John Salathé peers out of a chimney on
the first ascent of Sentinel's north wall.*

Allen Steck pounds a direct-aid piton
near the top of the north wall.

John Salathé posed for this snapshot on
the summit of Sentinel Rock after the
successful ascent.

dark cleft easily seen from the valley. This still remained the only possible way to the summit.

■ "The first sixty feet (the Headwall Lead) above the buttress is smooth, vertical granite. The Great Chimney is over a hundred feet to the left; it seems impossible to reach even by a tension traverse. Three hundred feet above the Chimney narrows down to less than a foot and the walls are bare and overhanging. You may get into the Chimney, but 'The Narrows' looks doubtful." Thus had Long and Bettler reported the situation at the top of the buttress. The Narrows seemed—and ultimately proved—to be the most spectacular lead on the entire wall.

■ As on the Arrow, the route here was unmistakably clear; we joked about who was going to be the first to make the terrible 150-foot swinging traverse into the Chimney, but it seemed unlikely that this was the easiest way. There were a few small water cracks leading up the head wall that looked "feasible," to use the word loosely. In June, Jim and I made the first all-out attempt on the wall. As charter members of the recently established "Berkeley Tension Climbers' Running Club," we conditioned ourselves for the five-day attempt by covering the standard cross-country course in the Berkeley Hills. But it was of little avail; on the first day a falling rock severed our rappel rope on the second lead and we had to retreat. Leaving our supply of water—two gallons—and some fruit up on the wall, we rappelled as best we could to the Tree Ledge.

■ On June 30, while the rest of the R.C.S. held its annual Minarets climbing trip, John Salathé and I climbed up to the Tree Ledge, prepared for another long siege. At the foot of the buttress we sorted our supply of hardware: fifteen carabiners, ten or so horizontal pitons, about eight angle pitons, and 12 expansion bolts plus hangers. We also carried a 300-foot rappel and a 120-foot quarter-inch hauling line for the packs, along with a little dried fruit. Our water, more dried foodstuffs, and a small can of tuna were up on the ledge 200 feet above, where Jim and I had left them.

■ Two days brought us over now familiar ledges to the small cairn on the buttress—800 feet, fourteen leads (all class 6 in part or in whole), and some eighty pitons later. From there on all was still unknown.

■ We were to be another two and a half days reaching the summit, only 700 feet above, but requiring eleven leads and some seventy-six pitons plus nine bolts. The upper part of the chimney is broken, and many of the leads were composed of short class-four stretches between class-six overhangs. The last lead to the summit was a 110-foot class-four "scramble."

■ On the entire four-and-a-half-day climb, thirteen leads were made by John and twelve by me. The ascent of this wall was probably the toughest one that either of us had ever made, or ever hoped to make again. Though John has 51 years to my 24, the climb seemed to have little effect on his endurance; only toward the end of the third day, did he seem to show signs of wear, but then both of us were ready to acknowledge the pleasures of simple back-country hiking. It was just too damned hot. Each afternoon at two the sun came from behind the wall and turned the face into a veritable furnace; temperatures up to 105° were recorded down in the valley and there wasn't a breath of wind. We could watch the swimmers down in the valley, languishing in the cool waters of the Merced—one would dive in now and then and we could easily see the white foamy splash as he hit the water.

The thought of suddenly finding myself in a cool fragrant spring was so maddening that it was hard to keep my balance. If only those swimmers would stop splashing! And this was only the third day! John never said much about it, but I knew he was thirsty. Standing there in slings, with his hammer poised over the star drill, John would turn his head and say, "Al, if I only could have just a little orange juice!" Up on that wall, oh what such a simple thing as a glass of orange juice would have been worth!

■ Inside the Great Chimney, I happened upon a little crack, glistening in the shadows. I remember watching, my lips tight and drawn, while a little bead of water seeped out and smoothly slid down the rock. It was barely enough to moisten my lips and wet my mouth, yet it was a wonderful sensation. We were so short on water that we could eat little during those five days. John left his dates in the chimney; he was tired of carrying them. I threw my food away upon reaching the summit. All in all I would guess that we ate half a pound of food apiece—as a liberal guess!

■ With ten expansion bolts already placed, the second ascent should do better, if there should ever be one. Six were needed on the Headwall lead. John stood in slings more than ten hours on that one. That day, the third, we made a total of only two hundred and forty feet. And after struggling over every foot of it, we were faced with the possibility of having to turn back. Not being able to go straight up, we climbed back into the chimney and eventually, through an inner chamber, reached a large ledge directly beneath The Narrows. Again the same old story—where to go? I can only say that there was little there with which to work. John finally made a bold attempt, using pitons upon which only he would ever rely (the double variety—back to back!); hanging almost horizontal, he was barely able to reach around to the outside of the chimney. The piton crack that he found made the lead. The Narrows were behind us!

■ The leads above here were agonizing in the hot sun. Still no wind. The packs got jammed in the chimneys, causing a great deal of wear on the nerves; there were bitter words, and we weren't afraid to let our tempers explode. When Ax Nelson heard of our plans, he remarked once to John, "If you expect to make the top, Al will have to be every bit as stubborn as you!" John agreed that I was.

■ The awful thirst. The overpowering heat cannot be described in simple words. Once on the top we could see the thin foamy line of the stream down in the gorge. We were on top, sure, but the ordeal wasn't over. We had yet to get down to the water that was staring us in the face. I slowed down for John as long as I could stand it, and then bolted down the couloir. I paid bitterly for my haste, for I descended into steep chimneys and had to claw my way back up through the hot dusty deerbrush looking for another way. My judgment was numbed by the thought of water. I tripped over bushes, fell over unseen ledges, and finally collapsed fully clothed into a pool at the foot of a small waterfall. This was the climax of the climb, a supreme climax! And I can say, in retrospect, that it was well worth the effort. The reason, the incentive, the motive for all this? It is an intangible, provocative concept that I shall leave to the reader to explain. Some think they know why; others despair of ever knowing. I'm not too sure myself.

THE NORTHWEST FACE OF HALF DOME

MICHAEL SHERRICK

[*Under the face of Half Dome is one of the most impressive spots on earth. El Capitan is higher; the Cathedral Spires are more like towers. But the awe of a single sheet of granite tapestry almost half a mile high and half a mile wide is unparalleled. The ascent of this face in 1957 put Yosemite on the mountaineering map. For the first time, climbers in Europe realized that Americans were developing a separate and at least equal brand of rock climbing. □ Several attempts were made in the years leading up to 1957. The successful party totally avoided publicity. They went so far as to time flashlight signals to their support party at the time of the Firefall, so that no tourists would see a light on the wall and create a sensation. This account was first published in the 1958* Sierra Club Bulletin. *□ The northwest face is the product of natural vertical joints in the granite. Lacking horizontal joints, the face cleaves in a way similar to a sheet of mica. A climber on the face becomes aware of current geological processes at work—so aware, in fact, that some climbers choose to protect themselves from rockfall by wearing helmets. □ In 1963 I was part of an attempt to climb a new route on this face. We failed, but one event left an indelible imprint on my memory. Several hundred feet above the base, the narrow crack in which we were inserting pitons widened. It became a chimney, large enough to crawl inside. At either side of the back wall of the chimney was a three-inch crack, continuing out of sight for hundreds of feet overhead. The back wall was eight feet behind the present surface, parallel to the main cliff. The cracks completely separated it from the outer rock, on which I was climbing. Here was the northwest face of the future, fully cleaved and waiting patiently, be it one or one hundred thousand years until it gleams for a geological moment in the noonday sun.*]—G.A.R.

■ IN THE eastern end of Yosemite Valley rises Half Dome, one of the scenic wonders of the United States. The summit of this huge granite monolith has been the goal of mountaineers, rock climbers, and hikers since 1850; the first ascent of the dome itself was done in 1875. The northwest side of Half Dome is a vertical face of smooth granite 2,000 feet high. On June 28, 1957, after five days of continuous climbing, Jerry Gallwas, Royal Robbins, and I made the first ascent of this wall.

■ As early as 1945 thoughts turned to this wall with the idea that a feasible route might be found. Climbers studied it with binoculars from the bottom and from the sides but it was discouraging, as anyone who has looked down from the top knows. In 1954 a Sierra Club party of Dick Long, Jim Wilson and George Mandatory climbed about 150 to 200 feet up from the base. In this same year other persons became interested in this climb; Jerry Gallwas, Warren Harding, and Don Wilson began some reconnoitering on their own.

29

The Vertical World of Yosemite

A telephoto view of the northwest face of Half Dome from Glacier Point.

They discovered that the broken bottom half could be climbed, and that there was a massive flake system ascending the top half of the face. The two problems were: (1) connecting the broken bottom half of the face and the flake system, thus making necessary a 300-foot diagonal traverse across a blank section of the wall (Robbins Traverse), and (2) going from the top of the flake system to the top.

■ In 1955 Jerry Gallwas, Warren Harding, Don Wilson, and Royal Robbins made the first major attempt. In three days they pioneered a route up 450 feet of the cliff using six expansion bolts, including one for a belay anchor, and one for a rappel anchor. With more knowledge of the problems and better equipment, this foursome hoped to return in 1956, but these plans failed to materialize.

■ On Saturday, June 22, 1957, Jerry, Royal, and I met in Yosemite Valley with plans for a second major attempt. We had assembled the best equipment available. We used nylon flight suit coveralls as outer clothing for Yosemite's comparatively warm bivouacs; underneath, a warm sweater over our regular climbing clothing. Polyethylene containers held our 13½ quarts of water (a little less than one quart per man per day). Food was kept to a minimum—a few cans of tuna, raisins, nuts, lemon juice, chocolate, and some particularly desirable packages of dates. We carried 45 pitons, including 18 horizontal pitons, 16 angles plus knife blades and wafers, and about 25 expansion bolts. We had more than 1,200 feet of nylon rope—two 120-foot 7/16-inch climbing, one 150-foot 7/16 climbing, two 300-foot 5/16 rappel, one 150-foot 5/16 hauling, and one 90-foot 5/16 hauling. Jerry Gallwas had forged about half of our horizontal pitons out of ChromeMoly steel alloy. These tough pitons survived a beating on almost every lead; some must have been used 15 to 20 times each. Jerry also made most angle pitons, which would fit cracks up to 2½ inches or wider; they too held up, despite being used perhaps a dozen times each.

■ Our gear was hauled up in a so-called torpedo bag which was girdled lengthways by 6 to 8 separate ropes for stability. The bag was covered with a duffle bag to minimize wear on the main parts. To prevent falling rocks as much as possible (usually thrown by someone from the top), Wayne Merry placed a sign halfway up the cables warning people against throwing stones because there were climbers below. We carried a first-aid kit and a flashlight. The latter was used to flash to the ground an elaborate system of prearranged signals at the time of the firefall. The time was chosen when people would be watching the firefall and we would attract less attention. Thus we make known our plans, progress and condition.

■ That Saturday evening we made the final arrangements with the park rangers, to whom we are indebted for their helpfulness. We packed our equipment into rucksacks in preparation for the next morning's pack in to the base of the climb. Wayne Merry volunteered to help us carry part of our equipment to the spot where we left the trail, after which he would climb halfway up the cables to place the warning sign.

■ On Sunday, June 23, after an uneasy night in our sleeping bags, the four of us shouldered our packs at Happy Isles and hiked up the Vernal and Nevada Falls trail where we took the branch which leads to the back side of Half Dome. Just before we came to the rock massif itself, we parted company with Wayne and proceeded down to the right along the base of

Using direct aid on the upper part of Half Dome's northwest face.

The first ascent party found this section of steep, almost flawless granite to be the most difficult on the climb. Repeated placement of pitons and modern equipment have eased the difficulty considerably.

Looking up the Half Dome face from the 500-foot level. The route follows cracks under the left side of the summit overhang.

the towering cliffs carrying the extra load. Late in the afternoon, desiring to get a good start, Royal and Jerry climbed about 150 feet up the cliff and left a fixed rope. Only the first 30 to 40 feet were 4th- and 5th-class; from there on it was mostly 6th-class climbing. We ate our supper cold, having brought no stove, and we bivouacked at the base of the cliff—our last contact with the ground for five days.

■ Monday morning, June 24, we packed the gear which was unnecessary for climbing, into the torpedo bag and filled our canteens from a small streamlet issuing from the rock. When all was ready, one of us started to prusik up the 150-foot rope and when he reached the top the second man would start. When the first two would be at the top of a pitch, they would haul up the torpedo bag, which at the beginning of the climb weighed 55 to 60 pounds. If the bag became stuck part way up the pitch the third man would free it on his way up the pitch.

■ From the top of this rope we followed the complicated route pioneered by the first attempt in 1954. It was all difficult, strenuous, 6th-class climbing; when we came to the first blank, slightly overhanging stretch, the bolts were already in place. Above the overhang we reached a small ledge with an expansion bolt for an anchor. In 1954 Warren Harding had climbed 50 feet from this ledge and had left another bolt from which to rappel at their high point, about 450 feet from the ground. We managed to climb another pitch before dark and reached a small sloping ledge about 500 feet above the ground where we spent our first uncomfortable night tied to the rock. The ledge was large enough, but it sloped down at an angle of about 20 degrees; any movement caused a tendency to slide off.

■ On Tuesday morning, June 25, the climbing became somewhat easier. By one o'clock we had ascended 400 feet of mixed, moderate 5th- and 6th-class pitches, generally less steep in angle, and arrived at the base of the "Robbins Traverse" about 900 feet above the base of the rock. From all past reconnoitering, this part looked to be the crux of the climb. We had to traverse an exceptionally blank wall for a diagonal distance of about 300 feet, with a vertical rise of about 125 feet, to reach a prominent series of chimneys and flakes ascending the center section of the cliffs. Our problem was to cross this traverse with a minimum of time.

■ Royal started at about one o'clock and found the first pitch not too difficult. A zigzag series of cracks led diagonally to a small ledge about 80 to 90 feet away, from which a belay was made. From this ledge a small crack led up the blank wall for about 30 to 40 feet where it ended in smooth granite. After eight pitons, a series of seven expansion bolts was placed with arduous hammer and drill work by Royal and Jerry. These brought Royal, late in the afternoon, to a meager network of cracks which led nowhere. After placing 3 pitons he descended about 50 feet on the 150-foot climbing rope and proceeded to attempt a long and difficult, not to mention "airy," pendulum traverse in order to reach a series of cracks about 40 feet to the right. After

Walking across "Thank God Ledge" near the top of the Half Dome route. The name came, not from the commodious nature of the ledge, as some unwitting climbers have assumed, but rather from the fact that the long ledge made possible an end run around the summit overhangs.

four attempts he finally reached a hold and placed several pitons in time to return, leaving a fixed rope, just before dark. We spent our second night out on the ledges at the foot of the Robbins Traverse, our most comfortable bivouac because we had ample space to sit.

■ On the third day, June 26, we retraced the previous afternoon's climbing on fixed ropes and proceeded up the crack to a small ledge where we placed an expansion bolt for an anchor. One more long 6th-class lead brought us to the large ledge of the great chimney system which was so apparent from the side of the rock. From the ledge a "fixed" rope was left tied securely to the highest expansion bolts to facilitate a retreat back across the traverse if one proved necessary. Let this serve as a warning to future parties: *it is* not *fixed on the top*.

■ At 10 o'clock we started up the beginning of a great chimney and flake system which was about 1,000 feet above the base of the climb. Some of these flakes were huge in size and either leaned against the rock leaving a crack, or were separated from the wall forming a chimney. The first large

Royal Robbins on the northwest face of Half Dome during the first ascent.

chimney ended in an extremely difficult chockstone about 80 feet above the base. Instead of climbing the chimney we took a straightforward 6th-class crack about ¾ to 1 inch wide which ran several feet to the left of the chimney. The flake was rejoined about 20 feet above the chockstone. From this point, strenuous 5th-class and some 6th-class stretches led to the top of the chimney system about 400 feet above us, 1,500 feet above the base of the climb. Of the pitches following the chockstone, one in particular deserves mention. Above the chockstone the chimney is filled with very large blocks of rock. One of them sticks out of the chimney about 8 to 10 feet at a distance of 6 inches from the wall. Royal led up about 40 feet, placing 4 or 5 pitons. At the bottom of this block with a secure piton in place, he grasped up underneath the inside edge of the bottom of the block with his hands and "walked" out the vertical face of the cliff, working his way up around the lip of the block to a belay stance some 20 feet higher. Several pitches higher, with darkness rapidly approaching, we bivouacked behind the last large flake of the chimney system, about 1,500 feet above the base and 500 feet below the summit.

■ The fourth day, Thursday, June 27, was the worst day. By this time lack of sufficient water, food, and sleep, plus the enervating hot sun rays had fatigued us. With Jerry doing most of the leading, we climbed only 300 feet, but we had to bivouac 50 feet below our high point in a small indentation sloping downward behind a flake. Although straightforward, this 300 feet was composed of extremely strenuous and tedious 6th-class climbing. In the morning we had left behind the part of the flake system where the flake was out away from the wall, giving a chimney effect. The flakes were now 3 to 7 feet thick and were flat against the wall leaving a crack ¹/₁₆ to 2½ inches wide. As the cliff was absolutely vertical, the climbing of the flakes followed a peculiar pattern; they would zigzag from left to right and back again across the face giving the effect of climbing one overhang of about 30 degrees for about 20 to 40 feet with angle pitons driven straight up, then up a 60-degree sloping ledge with pitons driven down for about 20 to 40 feet, and so on. This 250 feet of tedious work took almost a whole day. Before dark Jerry led an additional 50 feet, leaving his pitons for the next morning. That night was extremely uncomfortable, but we were exhausted enough to doze a good part of the time.

■ On Friday morning, June 28, we packed into the torpedo bag all our gear that was not necessary for climbing or safety and threw it out about 30 feet. It fell the full 1,800 feet to the base of the cliff without touching the rock! Although we were only 300 feet from the top, some of the most difficult 6th-class climbing was still ahead. Jerry retraced his steps and climbed to the end of the flake system about 100 feet above. There, to our luck, was a 50-foot "Thank God" ledge leading off to our left, saving us from the prospect of a blank wall leading up to a tremendous 150-foot overhang. This ledge was traversed by walking and hand traversing to a series of 6th-class cracks, which led up to the left-hand side of the base of the overhang, ending in a small ledge barely enough for us to stand on.

■ From this point, the obvious thing to do was to traverse to the left out from under the overhang. This led to one of the most crucial pitches of the entire climb. With a bolt for a belay anchor, Royal led outward on several very poor 6th-class pitons, and then placed 4 expansion bolts which led to a small ledge where the angle lessened considerably. Jerry then made a curving traverse along a shallow crack which led to some easy blocks just under the summit. We landed on top at 6:30 p.m.

■ Warren Harding was on hand to greet us at the top, whence we all proceeded down the cables. Warren went down to the valley while the three of us returned to the base of the climb to recover our equipment. Since it was too late to return to the valley before dark, we spent our sixth night out in our bivouac suits. Saturday, June 29, we returned to the valley and checked in with the park rangers, fortunate to avoid publicity about an accomplishment which would only have been made into a sensation.

■ Some have said that we did the "impossible," and it is unfortunate that for decades the word *impossible* has been such a common term in the mountaineers' vocabulary, being applied to that part of a mountain which presents an extreme in difficulty usually too demanding for the equipment and technique of the day. But improvements in technique and equipment just keep on happening.

EL CAPITAN

WARREN HARDING

[In 1955 Warren Harding and Royal Robbins climbed together in an attempt on the northwest face of Half Dome. They hoped to return in 1956, but that attempt never got off the ground. In 1957 Harding organized his own group and arrived in Yosemite to find Robbins' party well on their way to success. Harding hiked to the summit of Half Dome in time to meet the successful climbers. The next step after the face of Half Dome was obvious to him. He laid siege to the Nose of El Capitan. □ And so began one of the great ethical dilemmas of Yosemite climbing. Siege climbing: the use of fixed ropes. One group felt that unclimbed faces should lie dormant until ability and technique developed to a point where they could be climbed in "classic," or "Alpine," style—meaning in one continuous effort, such as the ascents of Sentinel's north wall and the face of Half Dome. The other group felt that since no climbers were capable of doing these routes without siege tactics, why not use them? The winner was obvious. One group was doing nothing on El Capitan and the other began to fix ropes over a period of 18 months. □ If fixed ropes were supposed to make the ascent easy, and enable climbers to eat steak in the Lodge every night, Harding never found the key. The final push on El Capitan was twelve days (without coming down). Harding spent the last 14 hours of the climb hanging on an overhang in slings drilling 28 bolts. He reached the summit at six in the morning. □ The climb provided some novel situations. Bill "Dolt" Feuerer designed specialized equipment which has never been used since. The Dolt Cart, which looked like a shopping basket with two bicycle wheels, was brought up to Dolt Tower, at the 1,200-foot level, by means of the Dolt Winch, a gadget attached to expansion bolts above the ledge. The motive power was human. The 1,200 feet of rope weighed far more than the payload. Tangles on the ledge in a single rope a quarter of a mile long were mind-boggling. Harding is not sure whether they were able to haul more food and water with the contraption than they consumed in the process of operating it. Forty-five days were spent on the wall. This account first appeared in the 1959 American Alpine Journal. *□ Today, during spells of good weather, one may find several parties climbing El Capitan at once. The Nose, however, was regarded with awe for quite a few years. Seven years after its first ascent, it had been repeated only three times. Now it is sometimes climbed three times in a month.]—G.A.R.*

■ I SUPPOSE this article could be titled "The Conquest of El Capitan." However, as I hammered in the last bolt and staggered over the rim, it was not at all clear to me who was conqueror and who was conquered: I do recall that El Cap seemed to be in much better condition than I was.

■ The above mentioned last bolt marked the conclusion of a venture that began in July, 1957. Mark Powell, Bill "Dolt" Feuerer and I met in Yosemite Valley intending to make an attempt on the North Face of Half Dome. We discovered that an excellent team of climbers from southern California was

El Capitan

already at work on it and had the situation well in hand. In our disappointment, we became a bit rash and decided to "have a go" at El Cap.

■ I'm sure no climber ever considered El Cap impossible—the term "impossible climb" having long since become obsolete. The fact that, previously, there had been no serious attempts to scale the sheer 2900-foot face was simply due to the common belief among rock climbers that techniques were not sufficiently advanced to cope with such a problem.

■ After we decided to attempt the climb, we spent an entire day studying the face in search of a continuous route to the summit. It is interesting to note that, on the climb, the route went exactly as we planned, with the possible exception of the "Roof Pitch," a formidable-looking overhang about 2000 feet up. I felt it would be best to bypass this obstacle, using a crack somewhat to the east. Later this crack proved to be only a water streak and we were forced to negotiate the "Roof."

■ It was obvious that existing methods of conducting a sustained rockclimb would be inadequate. Because of the extreme difficulty of the climbing we anticipated slow progress—perhaps no more than 100 to 200 feet a day. We would spend many days on the rock, so reasonably comfortable campsites were a necessity. Unfortunately there appeared to be very few ledges. We agreed unanimously that the only feasible plan of attack would be to establish a succession of camps up the face, linking them with fixed ropes. Supplies would be hauled up from the ground as needed. This would require a support party to assemble and tie loads to our hauling lines. Throughout the climb, such people as John Whitmer, Cookie Calderwood, Ellen Searby, and Beverley Woolsey contributed much to the success of the climb as they patiently plodded up the talus with loads of food and water. Our technique was to be similar to that used in ascending high mountains, with prusiking and rappelling gear replacing ice axe and crampons as aids for traveling, and winch and hauling lines instead of Sherpas.

■ On July 4, 1957, we began hammering our way up the smooth, glacier-polished wall. There was no thought of reaching the summit on this attempt—our tentative goal was El Cap Towers, the prominent pinnacles on the east side of the buttress about half way up the face.

■ On the third day we reached Sickle Ledge, 550 feet up, and established Camp I. The next four days were spent pushing the route upward toward the "Towers." The climbing was almost entirely 6th class, direct aid, and about as difficult as can be imagined. Finally, 150 feet short of the lower tower, we were forced to give up. Our special "stoveleg" pitons which had brought us up 300 feet of the two- to three-inch-wide "Stoveleg Crack" were so battered and flattened that they would no longer hold.

■ Leaving fixed ropes behind to secure what we had gained, we descended. Reaching the ground, our spirits were somewhat dampened by an unexpected problem. It seemed that our climbing presented quite a spectacle and had attracted a crowd of tourists which created a traffic jam at

Thunderheads boom over Yosemite, dwarfing the 3,000-foot face of El Capitan at the lower left. The first ascent route follows close to the left skyline of the cliff.

41

The winch in the above picture was used to haul equipment in the Dolt Cart, a strange bicycle-wheeled contraption never again to appear on the walls of Yosemite.

Warren Harding (left) and Mark Powell operate the Dolt Winch at the 1,200-foot level on El Capitan. Expansion bolts hold it to the wall above the ledge.

An expansion bolt placed in a hole drilled in granite. Although only a quarter-inch in diameter, the bolt will hold a force of more than a ton. It is attached to the rope by means of strong aluminum snap-links called carabiners.

George Whitmore prusiks up the final pitch on the first ascent of El Capitan, backlit by the setting sun.

Warren Harding leads the Great Roof on El Capitan as Rich
Calderwood belays in slings. When the leader cannot reach a ledge
in the length of his rope, he must make do by hanging from pitons
or bolts while the equipment is hauled and his companions move up.

Half way up El Capitan, Harding's sleeping bag was chewed through by rats, which apparently live on the wall by crawling up and down inside of large cracks. This picture was taken at Camp 4, 1,800 feet up the wall.

Harding during an early attempt on El Capitan.

A selection of hardware used on the first ascent of El Capitan. The pitons nearest the hammer were made by cutting the legs off junk stoves and crimping the tops.

The first continuous ascent of El Capitan, without fixed ropes, was made two years later. Here Tom Frost, Joe Fitschen and Royal Robbins (L to R) are bivouacked on Dolt Tower at the 1,200-foot level.

the road-junction near the base. The park rangers were understandably distressed and we had to agree to stay off the rock during the tourist season, between Memorial Day and Labor Day. This meant we would be climbing with shorter days and less certain weather. Difficulties of the El Capitan ascent were not confined to the rock!

■ According to our agreement, nothing was done until after Labor Day except to replace the many borrowed climbing ropes left as fixed line with a newly purchased half-inch manila.

■ Beginning with a four-day tour at Thanksgiving, there was a series of attrition attacks extending through October 1958 which whittled away the remaining 2000 feet to a point from which a final push might stand a chance of success.

■ Limited space prevents adequate description of the troubles and frustrations that plagued us in the next several months. About everything that could go wrong did.

■ The first, and probably worst, blow was Powell's unfortunate accident. In September 1957, he took a bad fall (while on an easy climb) and fractured and dislocated his ankle, putting himself out of action for a long time, if not permanently. Then, weather in the spring and early fall of 1958 was abominable. New equipment such as the winch, laboriously carted 1200 feet up to "Dolt Tower," was not nearly as effective as it might have been.

■ Along with the new equipment, new faces appeared on the rock. This, too, posed a problem. Powell and Feuerer felt that no new members should be admitted to the group. I didn't think the three of us constituted a strong enough party to go ahead on El Cap, since Powell, who had climbed brilliantly on the first attempt, was no longer capable of doing much leading. The dissension arising from this situation ultimately resulted in Powell and Feuerer dropping out, except for the continued use of Feuerer's pitons and other special equipment. So I continued with whatever "qualified" climbers I could "con" into this rather unpromising venture.

■ By mid-October 1958, Camp IV at 1800 feet and a high point at 2000 feet, just below the "Roof," had been established. The Chief Ranger had given us a deadline—to complete the climb by Thanksgiving. I have never understood how this was to have been enforced. But it didn't matter; we were all determined to reach the summit before winter.

■ After a long, hard look at the remaining 900 feet of the upper face, Wayne Merry, George Whitmore, Rich Calderwood, and I (who now made up the El Cap climbing party) agreed that an all-out effort was in order.

■ On November 1, 1958 we started up the fixed ropes for what we hoped would be the last time. The weather had cleared and the invigoratingly cool breezes were a pleasant contrast to the violent thunderstorms and oppressive heat of the nine-day effort in September. Due to a late start, we reached Camp IV a little after dark and were soon in our sleeping bags discussing plans for the next day's activities.

■ Next morning we ascended the fixed line to the previous high point and went to work on the long-dreaded "Roof Pitch." While strenuous and just a bit scary—nailing around the right side of the 180° overhang with 2000 feet of space directly below—it proved to be not nearly as difficult as we had thought it would be. The following seven days blurred into a monotonous grind—if living and working 2500 feet above the ground on a vertical granite face can be considered monotonous! On Sunday evening, the ninth day, a storm broke, providing a welcome day of rest from the hammering and hauling.

■ While sitting out the storm at Camp VI, snug in our sleeping bags with a rubberized nylon tarp warding off the wind and snow, Wayne and I took stock of the situation. Except for Rich Calderwood, who had gone down with an attack of nerves, we were all in good condition. Whitmore was somewhere below, most likely Camp IV, and would be coming up with another load of food. We had been working out of Camp VI for the past three days and, while we were not certain, we felt that our high point was surely no more than a couple of hundred feet below the rim. A determined push might put us over the top in one more day. We liked the thought, anyway. We were getting just a little tired of the whole thing.

■ By Tuesday morning the storm had blown itself out. After shouting our plans down to George, Wayne and I left Camp VI with extra food and batteries for our headlamps. Mid-morning found us at our high point and pushing on. As we began nailing up the next pitch, we heard a most welcome sound—a yodel from the top! John Whitmer, Ellen Searby, and Rick Anderson had hiked in to meet us. Spurred on by the encouraging knowledge that we actually were near the rim (because of the intervening

Wayne Merry relaxes on top of El Cap Towers, midway up El Capitan.

The vertical "Nose" of El Capitan stays bare of snow during winter storms.

overhangs, it had been impossible to see exactly where we were), we hammered up the next two pitches with enthusiasm if not speed. It was nearly 4 o'clock when we reached the tiny ledge that would serve as a belay-spot for the last pitch.

■ We could now see John and Ellen peering down at us. Also visible was the route between us and the top—a most impressive looking pitch! The first 60 feet was rather straightforward 6th class up a wide crack. The crack ended under an overhanging wall that was 90 feet high and completely devoid of cracks—15 pitons, 28 bolts, and 14 hours were required to surmount that final pitch. But at 6 the next morning I pulled over the top and stared feebly at Ellen as she struggled with her camera's faulty flash-attachment.

NOTES: The ascent took 45 days, spread over a period of 18 months. Although the face is 2900 feet high, so much altitude was lost due to numerous pendulum traverses, that a total of 3400 feet of climbing was necessary. About 675 pitons and 125 expansion bolts were used, 90 percent of which were for direct aid. The mileage of prusiking and rappeling has not been calculated.

El Capitan

A modern party on El Capitan give a victory salute from the beginning of the second pitch. They eventually retreated from high on the wall because of bad weather.

REALM OF THE OVERHANG

ALLEN MACDONALD

[*Unwittingly, the Leaning Tower is one of the most photographed rocks in the world. It appears in pictures taken from Valley View and the Wawona Tunnel Esplanade, two of the most famous views of Yosemite. But from these points the Leaning Tower is a formless wall to the right of Bridalveil Fall. To see the Tower in a spectacular perspective, one must stop at just the right place on the road, or else walk to a position where the profile of a thousand feet of constantly overhanging granite can be seen. □ My first climb in Yosemite was the relatively easy chimney south of the Leaning Tower. To approach the climb we walked under the overhanging wall. It was late summer in 1957. The "impossible" face of Half Dome had just been climbed. Serious attempts were in progress on El Capitan. But we viewed the Tower with an awe of a different sort. My companion pointed it out as a climb for a future generation. It seemed inconceivable that climbers would be able to ascend that smooth, mysterious wall. In 1961, only four years after our foretelling, the wall was climbed. □ The ascent was publicized in newspapers. TV cameras were lugged to the narrow ledge where the overhang began. The public accepted the climb as a step forward in American mountaineering. But climbers did not universally agree. Campfire sessions revolved around the ethics of big-wall climbing. How many bolts were justifiable to connect otherwise climbable sections of a route? Did fixed ropes make things too easy and take away much of the adventure? If limits are decided upon, just how are they to be enforced? □ Harding's answer to these questions is not printable. He felt then—and still feels today—that he is free to choose his own ways of climbing. To him it is a personal thing, not an institutionalized sport. Even as I write these words, I recall the gleam in his eye on a recent winter evening when he informed me that he planned to climb a blank wall near Half Dome. There is more to that gleam than simple anticipation of a new climb. □ The second ascent of the Leaning Tower's west face came a year and a half after the first. Royal Robbins soloed the route in four days. This was the first major solo climb in Yosemite. □ The account that follows was first published in the 1962* Sierra Club Bulletin. *It differs in style from many of the early climbing accounts in Sierra Club publications. It is the last of a genre—no articles on technical climbs have since appeared in these bulletins. The Sierra Club was outgrowing the era of a mountain outing club. It was fast becoming a national conservation organization in which fewer people knew about ropes and pitons. The slant of Macdonald's story reflects this change. It is the exact opposite of Anton Nelson's account of the Lost Arrow—written for prospective Arrow climbers. This was written for armchair mountaineers who might never be involved in climbing.*]—G.A.R.

The Vertical World of Yosemite

■ DAWN, on the last day of 1960, was cold, clear, and ominous. Although no snow had fallen, Yosemite Valley felt the hush of winter. The friendly burble of rushing water was gone. Bridalveil Fall hung in icy sheets, while the surrounding peaks retreated into silence, their smooth granite walls gray and cold. In these austere surroundings, we began one of the greatest adventures of our lives.

■ We were headed for the Leaning Tower. Only 1860 feet above the Valley floor, its height is not great by Yosemite standards. But height is only one measure of a mountain. The continuous overhang of the Tower's west face presents an extreme in difficult climbing. It might be compared to the Matterhorn in Whymper's day—a step beyond what any one had done. In the words of many climbers it was "for the next generation."

■ Considering the wall, we thought it seemed obvious that the ascent of the Tower would extend over many days, even weeks, causing supply and organizational problems encountered only in major mountaineering expeditions. A new method of climbing, introduced in the ascent of El Capitan's south buttress, would be required—expeditionary rock climbing.

■ Such a climb would also require a special type of leader. Without question, the perfect man for the job was Warren Harding, whose first ascents on El Capitan, the Washington Column, and many lesser known peaks are counted among the most difficult in the United States.

■ In the fall of 1960, Warren, ever in search of more daring struggles, turned his attention to the Tower's west face. The unattempted, seemingly unclimbable wall offered a challenge he couldn't resist.

■ Warren led off into the gloomy forest beneath the west face, his wiry body dwarfed under a huge pack. Next came Les Wilson, an old climbing friend of mine. I brought up the rear, following their intricate path through the giant talus boulders. The Tower loomed above us, massive and overpowering.

■ Across the valley, the top of "El Cap" was catching the first rays of light as we reached a small ledge that traverses the face, separating it into upper and lower halves. The lower wall is almost vertical; above the ledge, it bulges sickeningly out into space, overhanging the entire distance to the summit in one grand sweep. Above a stunted tree, 150 feet across the ledge, several small bolts (placed earlier by Warren) traced a line 60 feet high to a small roof. A rope, suspended from the topmost bolt, allowed us to ascend by prusik technique that portion of the wall already climbed.

■ Warren was soon ready for this airy trip up. With professional ease he stepped off the ledge to hang suspended 15 feet from the wall and 400 feet above the ground. He rose, rhythmically moving the prusik knots higher and higher, while a small breeze set the whole system, climber and rope, swaying like a giant pendulum.

■ In fifteen minutes he reached the high point where the serious climbing began up the right side of the roof. Placing pitons behind a very loose flake of rock, Warren found that each piton he put in threatened to dislodge the one below it, or worse, the flake itself. Finally, the crack ended and he changed to bolts. The angle at this point was more than 120 degrees. Warren worked tediously with Rawl drill and hammer. After twenty minutes of back-breaking work caused by the constant tension of the rope and back belt around his waist, he excavated a tiny hole one-inch deep and ¼-inch in

52

diameter. This effort was so exhausting that many times Warren would collapse quietly in his slings, head and arms hanging down in complete rest.

■ After pounding in a small expansion bolt, he gained three more feet. Above his head was another loose flake. In delicate balance, he carefully tested it. Deciding against pitons, he prepared to place another bolt, when without warning the flake broke off and crashed down on his head. Warren's angry and painful curses broke the silence.

"Warren. What happened? Are you hurt?"

A moan was the only reply.

■ I tied off the belay line and got out prusik slings. If he was unable to help himself we had only a short time to reach him before he would strangle in his own safety rope.

"Warren!" Les yelled again.

"My neck. I think it's broken."

"Do you want me to come up and lower you down?" I called.

"I don't know. Let me rest a second."

■ Small flecks of blood floated down. "You'd better go up, Al," Les said.

■ I got out my prusik slings and tied them onto the climbing ropes. What a mess, I thought. I knew how to effect a rescue having practiced it several times, but this was really a scary situation. The overhanging rock would complicate things and Warren was complaining on the way up about the difficulty of placing good bolts because of the hardness of the granite. Once I got up there, I wondered if the bolts would hold the two of us.

■ Fortunately, we didn't have to find out how bad the bolts really were. Warren regained his senses and was able to prusik down under his own power. We beat a cautious retreat and rushed Warren to the hospital where they stitched up a good-sized gash in his head.

■ This accident ominously ended our first attempt. While we were in high spirits at having escaped so easily, we realized that the Tower had won the first round.

■ **Second Attempt, June 17-24, 1961.** Heat, tourists, and smoke. That was Yosemite in June 1961. And I mean heat. It was the warmest we had ever felt it in the Valley. The Tower was just as forbidding as last December, but in a different way. Now it was the wall of an oven, reflecting heat and glare, painful to touch.

■ Saturday and Sunday, Warren and I, with the help of my brother in law, Chris Westphal, carried piles of equipment and supplies to the traverse ledge. It wasn't until Sunday afternoon that we actually continued the climb itself.

■ Warren again took the lead and bolted until after dark, ending the first pitch 135 feet up on an immense granite slab. He prusiked down, a small dark object silhouetted against the night, a creature from another world. We found the climb back across the ledge using the fixed ropes particularly exhilarating at night. The entire ledge is decomposing, and the frequency with which footholds dislodged and crashed hundreds of feet below made us particularly cautious. We worked our way down the talus using headlamps, and finally arrived at the ranger station at 11 p.m. We were a bit discouraged to find no word yet from George Whitmore, who was to be the third member of our party.

■ Nevertheless, on Monday Warren and I again climbed the talus, determined to force the route as high as we could. I was to belay in slings from the high point while Warren bolted above.

■ Taking a deep breath I pushed my chest prusik up and stepped off the ledge. Soon I was 25 feet from the wall. It was like being suspended from an airplane, a truly fantastic experience. When I reached the plumb line and began to rise, I started spinning like a twisted yo-yo. Warren, laughing like a madman, didn't help matters much. I discovered that if I concentrated solely on what I was doing and watched the rope right in front of me, the spinning wouldn't make me dizzy.

■ At the highest bolt I attached a wooden sling seat and was soon on belay to Warren. He came up and proceeded to pass over me in a tangle of ropes and slings. The overhang pushed both of us out, impressing us with the prospect of a 500-foot free fall to the talus. We started to laugh at what a ridiculous sight this must seem to the tourists watching from the Bridalveil Fall parking lot. It was rather strained laughter, though, as there was only one bolt holding the two of us.

■ Warren set to work at once. With tremendous endurance he pounded and pounded on the Rawl drill. The extreme overhang of the wall placed a great strain on Warren's feet and back, allowing him only ten or twelve strokes of the hammer before a rest. He also got cramps in his hands from constantly holding the drill above his head. Occasionally, during a rest period, Warren would haul up a plastic bottle filled with repulsively warm orange juice. All the while the sun seared into us, stifling desire and ambition. I found myself dozing on the belay. After what seemed an eternity, the sun reached the horizon and retreat for the night was in order. Our reward for the day—only 35 feet of burning granite.

■ That night, still no word from George. We met Glen Denny, a tall red-headed climber who had proved himself on the face climbs of Mount Conness and Keeler Needle. We didn't have to talk hard to persuade him to accompany us. Refreshed and encouraged by this piece of good luck, we slept at Camp 4 in hopes of an early start Tuesday.

■ In the morning, Glen and Warren started up the talus ahead of me as they would be climbing today. Our ascent was beginning to collect tourists like flies. One man, a tanned, bearded fellow, started up the talus behind me. It was George! At last the climbing party was complete.

■ Since George would be on the starting ledge, this gave me the day free to photograph and watch the climb from below like a tourist. Borrowing binoculars and eavesdropping, I had a very interesting and enjoyable afternoon. One older fellow had a telescope set up that could focus on Warren's ear—absolutely unbelievable. Comments varied from "crazy fools" to the most elaborate but erroneous descriptions of "what was going on up there." I was amazed at how misinformed most people are about climbing. Some actually believed that we stood on the ledge and threw the rope up the cliff, and that after the rope mystically attached itself to the rock, we pulled ourselves up hand over hand.

■ By Wednesday Warren had reached the end of the second pitch beneath a large overhang. The three bolts to which he attached the second fixed line were bad, and I decided to belay from the first anchor bolt. High above, Warren continued the lead, while George, below, started up the first fixed line to straighten out some tangled ropes. While adjusting my belay seat I noticed white dust on my pant legs. My anchor bolt had bent down and appeared to be coming out. I shouted a warning and quickly stepped up into a sling attached to the bolt above. George, hanging in space below, set an Olympic prusik record for descending.

■ With a wildly beating heart I watched Warren lower the bolt kit down on the hauling line. I placed another ⅜-inch bolt and tied the two anchors together. Everything seemed secure again.

■ Warren turned the overhang to the right and reached the beginning of a flaky crack where he ended the third pitch. I prusiked up the climbing rope and took out the bolts between us. We were short on bolt hangers and had to re-use them above. The bolts came out so easily I wondered if they would hold even a short fall.

■ It was 5:30 p.m. when, hot and tired, I reached the upper belay bolts. Sweat poured out of us and the warm orange juice couldn't quench our thirst. We decided against climbing on into the night and prusiked down.

■ Thursday, George and I awoke to sounds of tourists arriving in cars. News of the climb was really spreading. We met a television news photographer and carried his cameras to the beginning of the ledge where he spent the day photographing.

■ Above, Warren and Glen were hard at work on the flaky crack. Alternating pitons and bolts they climbed on through the day with the temperature hovering around 105 degrees. Since they were high up on the wall now, they decided to push on into the night and take advantage of the cooler hours. I waited at the traverse ledge by the hauling line, and George found a hole between two talus boulders 500 feet below. The acoustics were such that the climbing party could not talk directly to me, but we could relay messages with George as middleman. George promptly fell asleep, however, considerably confusing matters.

■ The night was beautiful—every star in sight. From above, the steady tap . . . tap . . . tap of bolts being driven kept me company. Garbled messages echoed off the buttress to the west. It wasn't until 3 a.m. that the noise stopped and I could lie down on the narrow ledge to catch a quick nap before morning.

■ Sometime that night, Warren and Glen had reached a sloping ledge they named "Guano" because of the birds' nests in the overhangs directly above. A 20-foot traverse to the left led to another ledge we called "Ahwahnee." Fortunately, Ahwahnee had dished-out sleeping places and was one of the best bivouac ledges we had ever seen. It was a monumental piece of luck and a real dent in the Tower's armor.

■ When I awoke Friday morning I climbed down to find George. After our short breakfast George yelled up to Warren, 1,000 feet higher, "What's it look like above?"

■ There was a long pause and a discouraging answer floated back, "It looks bad—real bad!" Our hearts dropped. Surely it couldn't be as hard as the portion we had just climbed. But above, the Tower's defenses multiplied—blank overhanging walls with small roofs jutting out here and there and near the summit a tremendous triangular overhang. If we could have tipped the Tower upside down it would have made an easy fifth-class climb.

■ George prusiked up with food and water and straightened out the

hauling lines, which had become horribly tangled during the night. I followed, taking out more bolts on the fourth and fifth pitches, arriving on Guano in the afternoon.

■ The exhausted faces that met me showed defeat. The wall above looked unbelievably difficult. We couldn't go on. The suffocating heat plus the strenuous climbing and logistical problems had beaten us. Glen and I prusiked down by nightfall, and Warren and George came down the next day. Warren had been leading during the last six days in terribly hot weather and climbing all night Thursday, truly an incredible show of tenacity and endurance.

■ To escape the heat we piled all the climbing gear in George's car and sped to Tuolumne Meadows where we sorted the equipment on the cool grass. After lunch we headed home. It would be three months before we struggled on the great wall again.

■ **Third Attempt, October 7-13, 1961.** With renewed enthusiasm we spent the weekend of September 30, 1961, getting ready for our next assault. Glen and I hauled supplies to Guano after ascending the fixed ropes we had left last June, while Warren tied on loads below. George, much to our disappointment, was unable to come because of business commitments.

■ With blistering hands we managed to pull up five heavy loads. Warren joined us on the ledge in the evening, and we spent a glorious night on Ahwahnee with a candle weirdly illuminating the ledge and casting giant shadows on the wall. We felt an immense sense of detachment and adventure—only a single nylon line connecting our world with the one below.

■ Warren had to leave for his home in Sacramento early Sunday morning, while Glen and I remained to rig a pulley system to ease the burden of hauling. When this chore was done we prusiked down (rappeling was impossible as the fixed ropes were pulled tight against the cliff to prevent our spinning on the way up) and reached Berkeley by dark, satisfied that we were ready for the big push, a week later.

■ The Tower's day of reckoning was approaching. We carried approximately 200 pounds of food and water as well as climbing equipment to the talus directly beneath Guano Ledge. Our food supply was composed of everything imaginable, including both canned and perishable foods from pomegranates to sardines. We took approximately 12 gallons of water, most of which we converted to Kool-Aid. Among the climbing equipment were drills, bolts, bolt hangers, all sizes of pitons, carabiners, 600 feet of 7/16-inch nylon climbing ropes and 1200 feet of ⅜-inch nylon hauling line. Ahwahnee Ledge fortunately was large enough to accommodate sleeping bags, so these were added to the list. All that remained was to get this huge mass up the wall to the upper ledges.

■ Warren and I prusiked up, towing the 1200-foot hauling line. The rope didn't even touch the cliff! It hung straight to the talus. When we were

Warren Harding prusiks the wildly overhanging first pitch of Leaning Tower.

ready to haul, Glen tied on a load and we tried to pull it up. It was no use.

■ "Too heavy! You'll have to lighten the load," we yelled down.

■ "There's only two gallons of water in it now," came the reply.

■ Hauling directly from the talus, about 1,000 feet, obviously wouldn't work. The weight of the rope, the load, and friction where the hauling line rubbed over Guano Ledge were more than Warren and I could lift. This meant Glen had to spend most of the night carrying loads 400 feet higher to the traversing ledge. Meanwhile, Warren and I, spending a comfortable night on Ahwahnee in sleeping bags, thought highly of Glen for his noble efforts.

■ It was clear, cold, and windy Sunday morning. Despite heavy clothing we almost froze getting ready to haul. Now it was Glen's turn to rest while Warren and I pulled thirteen loads up, almost covering Ahwahnee with supplies. Hauling is arm-tiring, exhausting work. Hand over hand . . . 25 feet . . . 50 feet . . . 75 feet . . . rest. Rope piles up on the ledge, making it difficult to move around. And finally, when you think you just can't pull any longer, a scrape is heard and a duffel bag with its small treasure appears over the edge.

■ That afternoon, while Warren was stocking Ahwahnee Ledge with food, a sudden gust of wind inflated my sleeping bag and flung it at him. He yelled and all but fell off the ledge getting out of the way. The sleeping bag, defying gravity, floated upwards 50 feet out from the Tower like a flying carpet, then collapsed and dove madly toward the talus below. Glen thought a giant rock had broken loose and was headed his way. The bag eventually landed 40 feet up a tree about 100 feet out from the base of the cliff.

■ When Glen joined us, my sleeping bag in tow, he found me belaying Warren on the sixth pitch. Typical piton-placing went like this: a poor angle, a ¼-inch bolt, a tied-off knifeblade, an angle behind an expanding flake, a Simond channel that shifted and bent in half. It was a most formidable pitch. At almost every piton came the casual warning, "This one looks pretty bad. Be ready." Warren finally reached a point 100 feet diagonally up and to the right of Guano Ledge. He placed a small bolt there and prusiked down the climbing rope to the ledge well after dark. Glen, flashlight in hand, lit our way across to Ahwahnee.

■ As we had neglected to bring a primus stove with us, we had no warm meals. Sunday the main course was cold ravioli.

■ The next morning Warren resumed his lead with Glen belaying. Climbing a large deep crack using bong-bongs, he reached a belay stance on a small sloping foothold. It seemed like a ledge to us. We rated the pitch as severe sixth class taking 34 pitons, three ¼-inch bolts, and eight hours to lead. Because this pitch was diagonal, the prusik was almost horizontal for some distance, placing a good strain on rather doubtful anchor bolts.

■ Glen had some trouble following Warren's lead, because a few of the pitons came out in his hand before he could step up on them. Nonetheless, he soon reached Warren and continued the lead diagonally left on six pitons, most of them knifeblades, and three tiny ³/₁₆-inch bolts. Darkness crept up the wall, bathing the Tower in splendid alpenglow, as Glen and Warren set up the ropes for retreat.

■ An early breakfast Tuesday morning meant that I was on belay before 8:30 a.m. Glen finished his lead, placing eleven more ³/₁₆-inch bolts. At the end of the pitch he placed a good ⅜-inch bolt. For once the bolt drove in well, and the large flake of rock it was imbedded in seemed solid, too. A fixed rope was installed from this bolt to Guano Ledge 200 feet below.

■ Following this pitch I found that Glen, who is quite tall, had spread the pitons and bolts extremely far apart. Later, Warren and I talked about designing a "Denny-Arm," a device allowing you to make the absurd reaches prerequisite for anyone who follows Glen on a sixth-class lead. We left the bolts in on this pitch, but removed the hangers to re-use above. After reaching Glen, I was able to rappel down the rope 180 feet before prusiking into the ledge became necessary (a distance of about 25 feet). It was a wild free rappel, however, and we stuck to prusiking during the remainder of the climb.

■ Humor often built up to epic proportions. Warren's taciturn ways seemed to give him an oriental personality, and our laughing often revolved around his antics. Rarely a moment went by when one of us wasn't laughing at something.

■ From our high point on Tuesday, an overhanging "open book" filled with mud and weeds led onward, blocked from time to time by small roofs. On Wednesday I belayed in slings while Warren placed 29 pitons of moderate sixth class. The "Garden Pitch" was an appropriate name for this section. Warren would laugh and say, "Close eyes, please," as large masses of dirt and foliage rained down. A big, loose block of rock at the end of this section presented a problem. Somehow Warren managed to push it off. We could see the ground clearly and were sure no one was beneath the block. We also took the precaution of yelling "Rock" several times before we let it go. Warren, however, was yelling "Lock!", which again tied Glen and me in stitches. The huge slab whooshed past, 15 feet from the wall, and plummeted 1100 feet to the talus below. The loud crash echoed across the Valley. I removed the pitons from the pitch and we returned to Guano Ledge, dirty and worn out.

■ We were all getting tired of the cold food. Stew was on the menu for tonight. It had almost no taste and a cold, slimy feeling in my mouth. I ate very little, but Warren and Glen, having much sturdier stomachs than I, finished it off to the last drop. We passed another star-filled night telling climbing stories, and the party remained in high spirits.

■ Thursday was my rest day. Lying on my back on Ahwahnee Ledge, I soaked up sun and enjoyed the pleasurable experience of watching Warren and Glen climbing hundreds of feet above—a delicate ballet in air of two superb climbers.

■ Glen led a short, vertical pitch ending under the large triangular roof which is clearly visible from the Valley floor. This we were sure would be another crucial section. Warren took the lead. He was now climbing parallel to the ground in the most acrobatic fashion. The large bong-bong pitons he pounded in made strange music to accompany this impressive sight. The angle eased as he passed the outer edge of the roof. It was very strenuous sixth class. He climbed free the last 25 feet to two sloping ledges—the only portion of the climb made without direct aid.

■ Night was almost upon us. The Valley was already in shadow. From our separated points—Warren and Glen 500 feet above my spot on Ahwahnee Ledge—we held a council of war. We decided to bivouac on the tiny upper ledges, anticipating the summit the next day.

■ The sun was just setting as I hastily threw some dried and canned apricots, fruit juice, flashlight, and clothing into a hauling bag and cleaned up Ahwahnee Ledge. After a last look at this fabulous place that had been our home for so long, I began the long prusik up. In a relatively short time I reached the bottom of the overhang and remained there in slings while Glen cleaned the pitons out of the roof. He finally reached Warren and they tied off the prusik rope. After another delay they were ready to haul up the sack. I dropped the line with the sack attached; it flew out incredibly far from the wall before disappearing in the darkness.

■ I then began one of the most frightening prusiks I have ever done. The rope dropped down from me, went straight out past the lip of the overhang and ascended into the blackness beyond. I was even confused as to how to start. I put an extra prusik loop in my mouth, more to bite on to ease tension than anything else. My mind was numb from trying to calculate the strain I would be placing on the system. If I could just be sure everything would hold! Finally, I realized there was nothing else I could do, and soon I was in my slings dangling 30 feet out from the wall.

■ The headlights of cars were an infinite distance below as they turned and twisted along the road. I couldn't help thinking about the tourists inside. What a contrast—tomorrow they might be swimming in the Merced River or taking pictures of El Capitan and Yosemite Falls, while we would be struggling upward, reaching for the top and the culmination of our climbing careers. And all within sight of one another. I finally reached the ledges and found the rope tied off to a small ¼-inch bolt and two doubtful pitons. I shuddered when I thought of the strain I had just placed on them.

■ We spent a long, cold, moonlit night under attack by small birds. The apricots and Lifesavers (a very appropriate name) helped stave off hunger pains. No comfortable ledge like Ahwahnee this time, and no sleeping bags either. Warren told us that the route above looked like easier climbing, maybe fifth class. The overhanging open book that greeted us Friday morning proved him wrong.

■ Warren led the last pitch, overhanging to the end, up fairly difficult sixth class, using 20 pitons and 5 bolts. Glen cleaned the pitch of pitons and I made the last prusik to the beautiful summit arête.

■ And then we were up. The struggle was over and the Tower was ours.

■ Our first feeling was one of intense happiness, bubbling up inside so we felt like shouting for pure joy. This soon gave way to deeper emotions: a contentment that we had savored life at its fullest for a short while—a life stripped to barest essentials. No matter what the future held for each of us, the Tower had linked us in a bond of comradeship that most people never experience. We'll always feel respect and affection for that wall.

■ As we climbed down the sloping back side of the Tower, the soft play of afternoon sun and shadow gave a nostalgic beauty to the area. Between the Cathedral Rocks we paused for a last look at our huge granite friend, then plunged down into the dark depths of Gunsight Gully to a new world waiting below.

THE SALATHÉ WALL EL CAPITAN

ROYAL ROBBINS

[Harding's route up The Nose is the boldest line up El Capitan. In contrast, the Salathé Wall is the most devious—traversing, arcing and even rappelling on its lower half. But the reason for the devious appearance is that the Salathé Wall follows the chief line of weakness on El Capitan. In the opinion of many top climbers, it is the greatest rock-climbing route in the world. □ *A large percentage of the route is free climbing at a high standard on superb granite. Where the original ascent of The Nose required 125 expansion bolts, only 13 were used on the Salathé—all on the lowest fifth of the route. The climb was made in a compromise between siege and Alpine styles. Fixed ropes were used on the first ascent for the first third only. Two members of the party, Royal Robbins and Tom Frost, returned a year later to make the first continuous ascent without fixed ropes. The article we publish here first appeared in the 1963* American Alpine Journal. *Because of the great beauty and importance of this route, we have weighed heavily on photographs, using more than in any other chapter.]—G.A.R.*

■ OUR muscles tensed when we heard the air rushing across the rock face. Seconds later we were rudely buffeted by an incredibly strong and ferocious blast of wind. We worried lest our excellent Austrian bivouac sack should tear and leave us completely exposed to the elements. The wind blew in appalling gusts almost continuously, with occasional short periods of dead calm. Rain fell steadily, and whenever the wind died, the natural drainage asserted itself and we received a waterfall directly upon our heads. This tempest had been pounding us for five hours. It was midnight in mid-October, 1962. Tom Frost and I were curled on a long, narrow ledge, 2700 feet up the southwest face of El Capitan, otherwise known as the Salathé Wall.

■ The reasons for our being in such an unlikely place at such an unlikely hour are connected with an event which occurred on November 12, 1958. On that day Warren Harding, Wayne Merry, and George Whitmore completed the first ascent of the south face of El Capitan. In doing so, they established an elegant and impressive route directly up the Nose of the monolith. They used 3000 feet of fixed ropes, several hundred pitons, 125 bolts, and 45 days of climbing spread over a period of a year and a half. Two years later four young Californians, Joe Fitschen, Tom Frost, Charles Pratt and I, made the second ascent, which, in its own way, was also a major first ascent. It was the first continuous ascent of the route (i.e. no returning to the ground before the ascent is finished), accomplished in seven days. This single-push ascent was made possible through knowledge of the route and utilization of the expansion bolts which had been placed by Harding and his companions.

61

The southwest face of El Capitan. The Salathé Wall begins near the shadows in the lower right and diagonals upward to the "Heart," the 800-foot-high, heart-shaped depression below and right of the center of the wall. Dropping to the bottom of the "Heart," the route follows near the left lobe and eventually makes a direct line toward the summit. There are, at this writing, nine other routes in this photograph.

*Royal Robbins leading difficult friction climbing on the first day of
the Salathé Wall.*

■ The Salathé Wall is neatly separated from the southeast face by the Nose
of El Capitan which juts boldly into Yosemite Valley. In September, 1961,
Chuck Pratt, Tom Frost, and I made the first ascent of the Salathé Wall. This
precipice received its name in commemoration of that great pioneer of
modern American rock-climbing, John Salathé. Our route starts just 100 feet
left of the Nose and traverses west for hundreds of feet to "Hollow Flake
Ledge" at the 1100-foot level, whence we ascended in a very direct line to
the top of the rock. Although the first ascent of the Nose had required a
prolonged siege with thousands of feet of fixed ropes, we wished to avoid
such methods if possible so as to keep the element of adventure high with
at least a moderate amount of uncertainty. It was perfectly clear to us that
given sufficient time, fixed ropes, bolts and determination, any section of
any rock wall could be climbed. To remove this certitude which tends to
diminish our joy in climbing, we had planned an attempt involving two major
efforts. The first was three-and-a-half days long and took us across the long
traverse to "Lung Ledge", 900 feet above our starting point. From here we
descended to the ground on fixed ropes and returned several days later for
the second stage: an all-out effort to finish the climb. We prusiked up,
removed our fixed ropes and went for the top, which we reached after 6
days of the most rewarding climbing we had ever done. Altogether, in
nine-and-a-half days of climbing, we placed 484 pitons and 13 bolts.

The Salathé Wall does have some large and comfortable ledges.
Here Chuck Pratt coils a rope on Heart Ledge.

■ In September, 1962, with Pratt in the Army, Frost and I returned with TM Herbert to attempt a continuous ascent of the wall. Yvon Chouinard and Steve Roper had already attempted such an ascent in the spring of this same year, but after a rapid and auspicious beginning, they were forced to descend because of a badly worn hauling bag.

■ Since we started rather late in September, we had reason to expect cool weather. However, we suffered considerably from July-like heat during the first two days. Also, I contracted a vague but debilitating sickness, which caused me to feel exhausted after small efforts. By the end of the second day we were settling down for a bivouac on Hollow Flake Ledge, which lies at the end of the traverse, 1100 feet up. Our high point that day had been 1400 feet, 300 feet above our bivouac. The sky had become completely cloudy two hours before nightfall, and as we lay supine and exhausted early in the evening, we implored whatever meteorological deity there might be to send water to restore our desiccated bodies. Whenever a cloud came over which looked as if it might drop some moisture, we opened our mouths and stuck out our tongues, hoping to catch any drops that fell. We need not have

Climbers nearing the top of Lost Arrow Spire.

65

El Capitan dominates this view of Yosemite Valley in winter.

Waiting out a storm on El Capitan during the first ascent of the North America Wall.

Warren Harding during the first ascent of the south face of Half Dome.

Free climbing a long jam crack on Reed Pinnacle.

69

Free climbing an undercling on Peter Pan, ⸻ ⸻mb on the lower part of El Capitan.

El Capitan during the clearing of a storm.

Don Lauria holds a skyhook in his bruised and blackened hands after the second ascent of the North America Wall on El Capitan.

On the second pitch of the Salathé Wall, the upper headwall leans
ominously overhead.

73

A tension traverse above Heart Ledge. Originally climbed with just pitons, this pitch has now been graced with an expansion bolt where early parties found it unnecessary.

Chuck Pratt liebacks a crack on the first ascent of the Salathé Wall.

TM Herbert climbs the Hollow Flake Crack during an unsuccessful bid to make the first continuous ascent, without fixed ropes.

bothered, for our prayers were more than answered that evening; indeed, at the risk of impiety I would venture to say the rain god showed a lack of good judgment in the filling of our verbal requisition. A grey wall of cloud advanced toward us. In a few minutes three inches of hail had fallen on the ledge and we were shoveling it into our parched mouths as fast as we could swallow. The water began to run down the wall and we ran around, Charlie Chaplin-like, filling our water jugs with what turned out to be an evil liquid, sediment-filled and bad tasting. Violent and prolonged downpours continued all night and were accompanied by brilliant electrical displays and consequent fulminations which reverberated up and down the valley. It was an exciting, if sleepless night; a night fit for King Lear.

■ We spent most of the next day, a clear sunny one, sleeping. We were physically spent and in no mood for climbing. TM was now suffering from an enervating illness similar to mine, but we thought a day of rest and considerable water might enable us to recuperate sufficiently to finish the climb. Unfortunately, much of the water we had collected was so putrid as to be undrinkable. On the fourth morning we scarcely felt better and descended. This required many hours of cautious and methodical work and involved a long and delicate pendulum from our high point at 1400 feet to regain horizontal distance to Lung Ledge, whence we could rappel to Heart Ledge and so to the ground.

■ The next attempt to make a continuous ascent occurred in October. TM had returned to southern California, and so Tom and I were alone. We were taking a closely calculated risk this time and carrying a minimum of food, water, and equipment. We limited ourselves to thirteen quarts of water, five of which were already on Hollow Flake Ledge from the previous attempt. As the event proved, we could easily have managed on ten quarts, and we were to pour out over two quarts near the top. In addition to the limited amount of water and food, we carried 50 carabiners, 60 pitons, the equivalent of a heavy sweater apiece for warmth, and a marvelously light and durable Sporthaus Schuster bivouac sack. We dispensed with a camera this time and did not carry a bolt kit.

■ As we started climbing early on October 10, the sky was clear and the temperature cool. There was as yet no sign of the forecasted rain. However, later in the morning, clouds, fragments and clumps of nimbo-stratus, began moving swiftly from the south and it looked as if the Weather Bureau, which had been unsuccessfully forecasting rain for several days, might finally be right. As the clouds scudded over our heads toward the north, Tom skillfully led the difficult section of the blank area where we had placed thirteen bolts the previous year. The use of more bolts in this area had been originally avoided by some enterprising free climbing on two blank sections and some delicate and nerve-wracking piton work. It would take only a few bolts to turn this pitch, one of the most interesting on the route, into a "boring" walk-up.

TM Herbert climbing difficult (5.9) face climbing. To this day his friends are unsure whether he was clowning or scared when this picture was taken.

Steep direct-aid climbing above Hollow Flake Ledge.

Behind El Cap Spire, a free-standing pinnacle.

Chimneying out of the Ear, a horrifying bomb bay halfway up the climb.

Looking down on the top of El Cap Spire. Royal Robbins rests on its level summit.

Chuck Pratt leads direct aid above El Cap Spire.

■ As the clouds thickened we climbed around the well-known "Half Dollar" and up to Mammoth Terraces, 1000 feet above our starting point. We then climbed down 50 feet and rappelled 150 feet to Heart Ledge, at the base of a large heart-shaped recess which is one of the conspicuous features of the wall. From Heart Ledge I led the next pitch to Lung Ledge. Following this, Tom made a thrilling pendulum and then struggled up a jam crack for 120 feet to Hollow Flake Ledge. This difficult pitch had been led by TM Herbert on the previous attempt. Darkness fell as I followed Tom's lead; rain appeared imminent.

■ To our surprise, no rain fell that night, though the morning sky on the second day was still mostly cloudy. We had no problem with heat and forced ourselves to drink water to eliminate excess weight. After several hours of mixed free and direct-aid climbing that second morning we reached the "Ear", a large flake which had caused us considerable trouble and delay on the first ascent. We had lost several hours then in a fruitless attempt to bypass this frightening formation, but finally attacked it directly. This involved using chimney technique to move 30 feet horizontally behind the flake, with the bottom of the flake yawning abruptly into space—an unnerving procedure. Tom led this anxiety-producing pitch with nearly perfect composure—only a few screams of terror and moans of horror. I nailed 150 feet to a small ledge, and thence a fiercely difficult jam crack brought us to the base of El Capitan Spire, an 80-foot Lost Arrow-type pinnacle separated from the wall by only a few feet of space. A shower and strong winds hit us here and more of the same seemed certain. We chimneyed to the top of the spire and I then led 75 feet of the next pitch. We spent the night on top of the spire, 1800 feet up. The sky was filled with clouds and a strong wind blew from the south, but again we passed a night without receiving the expected downpour.

■ The next day brought more of the same weather, which was excellent for climbing: cool, stimulating and though threatening, only threatening. By nightfall of the third day we had climbed 2500 feet and were faced with an important decision. We could rappel 150 feet to a good ledge below and bivouac or we could attempt to continue after dark in an effort to reach "Sous Le Toit Ledge", 60 feet away horizontally and around a large bulge in the face, beyond a long and complicated pitch which includes a pendulum. After mentally weighing the factors we decided to continue climbing—a lucky decision as it turned out. A full moon was shining so brightly that we received considerable light through the clouds and seldom used our single flashlight. We reached "Sous Le Toit Ledge" at 11:30 p.m. and settled down for a chilly bivouac. The weather signs still portended rain or snow. With all these clouds moving in from the Pacific there must be *something* out there. How long would it hold off?

■ On the morning of the fourth day we ascended a long and interesting pitch to a 20-foot overhang called the "Roof". Surmounting this roof, which was composed of several tiers, each overhanging the one below, involved some of the most spectacular and strenuous climbing on the route. Above the roof was a 200-foot overhanging headwall. The climbing on this headwall was all direct-aid, very difficult in several spots, and slow. All day, as we climbed, the wind blew in gusts of startling strength. We could see how it passed over the trees below as one normally observes its action on tall grass

At the lip of "The Roof" on the Salathé Wall, a 20-foot tiered overhang.

Looking down through the belayer's
legs from above "The Roof."

Curving folds of overhanging granite
near the top of the Salathé Wall.

A short but severe overhang on the
Salathé Wall. Note how the piton
placements become closer together as
the angle steepens.

A hanging belay on the 200-foot headwall above the roof. Use the dangling ropes to judge the angle of the rock.

Layton Kor, a prolific climber of the Sixties, at the top of the Salathé Wall.

or a field of wheat. Belaying in slings, we were violently blown this way and that, and the wind's force made it difficult to stand high in our slings to place pitons.

■ We were both up on "Thank God Ledge" by nightfall, just in time to prepare for the rain, which the wind drove on us all night. Just before dawn a little snow fell on the ledge, while on top of the rock, 300 feet higher, three inches lay on the ground. At daybreak we forced ourselves out of our sack. With considerable effort we ate, and drank a little water. The precipitation had ceased and the storm passed to the southeast. Numbed, we climbed slowly that morning, but by the time we finished the first pitch the sun shone upon us from an almost clear sky. Water ran down the face from the melting snow above and Tom was hit by a piece of ice. The last pitch was a fitting climax to the climb. On the first ascent Chuck Pratt had led this pitch. On that day I was prusiking and hauling, but Tom had followed Chuck's lead and came up sweating, cursing, and praising Chuck's uncommon talents.

■ We finished the climb in magnificent weather, surely the finest and most exhilaratingly beautiful Sierra day we had ever seen. The air was cool, but the direct sunlight was warm and friendly. All the high country was white with new snow and two or three inches had fallen along the rim of the Valley, on Half Dome, and on Clouds Rest. One could see for great distances and each peak was sharply etched against a dark blue sky. We were feeling spiritually very rich indeed as we hiked down through the grand Sierra forests to the Valley.

Bishop's Balcony, a spectacular direct-aid practice climb. The original ascent used pitons of knifeblade thickness, while today's climbers use pitons over an inch wide in the well-worn grooves.

MODERN YOSEMITE CLIMBING

YVON CHOUINARD

[*Much has changed in the decade since Yvon Chouinard wrote this article for the 1963* American Alpine Journal. *Then Yosemite climbing was almost entirely the province of an elite group of California climbers. Even though ascents on El Capitan and the Leaning Tower had received considerable publicity, most climbers in Europe and North America were unfamiliar with Yosemite techniques. Chouinard addressed this article to that audience.* □ *In the same year this article was published, the first* Climber's Guide to Yosemite Valley *was also published. By 1965 Yosemite had visitors from many different regions climbing at a high standard. Today it seems a majority of climbers in the Valley are from out of state. During the transition, printed matter about Yosemite climbing was at a premium. Would-be Yosemite climbers hung on every word. Chouinard has a habit of making all-encompassing statements. To his friends, his sweeping generalizations are just part of his dynamic personality. Some of his readers have tried to follow him to the letter.* □ *Four or five years after this article came out, I was having a beer with a climber from the East. He began talking about Tahquitz Rock in southern California. I broke in and said that I had never done a route at Tahquitz. Typed words could never express his look of incredulity. Every year he had spent a week at Tahquitz before going to Yosemite. Chouinard had written in his article: "Every spring even the native climbers spend a week at Tahquitz getting in shape for the Valley walls."* □ *One of Chouinard's predictions was deadly accurate. He realized the limited possibilities of big new climbs in Yosemite. And he predicted that "The future of Yosemite climbing lies not in Yosemite, but in using the new techniques in the great granite ranges of the world."*]—G.A.R.

■ YOSEMITE climbing is the least known and understood and yet one of the most important schools of rock climbing in the world today. Its philosophies, equipment and techniques have been developed almost independently of the rest of the climbing world. In the short period of thirty years, it has achieved a standard of safety, difficulty and technique comparable to the best European schools.

■ Climbers throughout the world have recently been expressing interest in Yosemite and its climbs although they know little about it. Even most American climbers are unaware of what is happening in their own country. Yosemite climbers in the past have rarely left the Valley to climb in other areas, and conversely few climbers from other regions ever come to Yosemite; also, very little has ever been published about Yosemite. Climb after climb, each as important as any done elsewhere, has gone completely unrecorded. One of the greatest rock climbs ever done, the 1961 ascent of the Salathé wall, received four sentences in the *American Alpine Journal*.

■ Just why is Yosemite climbing so different? Why does it have techniques, ethics and equipment all of its own? The basic reason lies in the nature of the rock itself. Nowhere else in the world is the rock so exfoliated, so glacier-polished, and so devoid of handholds. All of the climbing lines follow vertical crack systems. Every piton crack, every handhold is a vertical one. Special techniques and equipment have evolved through absolute necessity.

■ **Special Problems.** Since Yosemite has characteristics all of its own, it also has its special problems and difficulties. Because the Valley lies at an altitude of only 4000 feet, the cliffs are often covered with trees and bushes, and the cracks are usually filled with dirt and grass, making it more difficult, time-consuming and uncomfortable for the first ascent party.

■ Situated in the center of sunny California, the threat of stormy weather is not serious; however, when an occasional storm does hit, usually in the spring or fall, it can be serious because most climbers are not prepared mentally, physically, or materially for it. American mountaineers have tended to belittle the climbing in Yosemite because of the fact that it lacks the storms of the high mountains, but personally I have never suffered so much from the weather as I have in Yosemite.

■ Bad weather in California means hot weather. The usual climbing temperature is 85° to 90° during the day and 50° at night. Temperatures above 100° are common. During June and July of 1961 there were fifteen consecutive days with temperatures of over 95°! It is usually too hot to do much climbing from late July to the first of September. The heat poses a related problem, that of carrying great loads up the walls. The *minimum* water that must be taken on the big climbs is 1½ quarts per man a day. Water, food and bivouac equipment, combined with the usual 45 pitons and 35 carabiners, make a considerably heavier load than one carried on a comparable climb in the high mountains. On a two or three-day climb, the second man climbs with a fairly heavy pack, while the leader hauls up another. The latter always has two ropes, one to climb with and the other to haul up extra pitons or the pack.

■ **Safety.** Even with the standard of extreme difficulty which has been achieved, safety has not been disregarded. There are many reasons for this, the most important, of course, being the American's love of safety and security and his innate fear of death, which have caused revolutionary innovations in belaying and equipment. Pitons are used far more numerously for protection than in Europe. Objective danger is also less in Yosemite than anywhere else in the world. There is little danger of natural rockfall, loose rock or bad storms; as the rock is so smooth and steep and has few ledges, a fall usually only helps to build one's confidence.

■ **Free Climbing.** Not only is every piton crack vertical, but nearly every handhold is a vertical one. Lay-backing, jamming, chimneying, pinch-holds and friction climbing are the usual techniques. Face climbing, such as one finds in the Tetons or the Rockies, is a rarity.

■ Most persons who have never climbed in the Valley are under the impression that the rock is similar to that in Chamonix or the Bugaboos. This is not so. They have completely different types of rock. Yosemite granite does not fracture in angular blocks as does the granite of the French Alps or even the rest of the Sierra Nevada. The Valley is actually a series of exfoliation domes that have been cut in half by a river and glaciers. This means that most of the climbing is on flakes, be they small and thin or large dihedrals. Pitons are placed almost always behind a flake or in a vertical inside corner. This vertical-crack climbing takes not only a great deal of technique but also enormous strength. Yosemite climbers develop certain characteristic muscles as a direct result of using vertical holds.

■ There is undoubtedly more chimney climbing in Yosemite than in any area in the world. Chimneys range from those that require one-arm and one-leg techniques to others that have chockstones bigger than a house, from perfect "Rébuffat" types to flaring, bomb-bay, horizontal "horror" chimneys, and from short slots to some that are over 1000 feet high. Also characteristic of the Valley is friction climbing on glacier-polished slabs. There are climbs in the Valley that have hundreds of feet of this. Very difficult moves have been made on these slabs, using friction, fingernail holds, and edging on tiny flakes. These must be treated as if one were only a few feet off the ground because the second one loses confidence, even for a moment, hands sweat, legs shake, feet slip—and one is out in space.

■ All the techniques of free climbing were established not in Yosemite but at Tahquitz Rock in southern California. From the 1930s to the present day, it has been the training ground for nearly every prominent Valley climber. This magnificent rock has over seventy routes on massive, exfoliated granite, similar to Yosemite's except for its lack of glacial polish and dirt in the cracks. This means that a move will go free at Tahquitz where normally in Yosemite it would require direct aid. Because of its accessibility, compactness and sound piton cracks, Tahquitz offers ideal conditions for pushing free climbing to its limits. Most of the routes were first done with direct aid, but over a period of time nearly every one has been done free. It was the first area to have class 5.9 climbs and continues to have the greatest concentration of class 5.8, 5.9 and 5.10 routes in the country.

■ When one finds a lay-back or a friction pitch at Tahquitz, it is a textbook-type pitch; a lay-back is a pure lay-back requiring pure lay-back technique, a friction pitch requires pure friction technique. Nothing else will do. One can develop granite-climbing technique here far better than in Yosemite or anywhere else. I can not impress it enough on climbers from other areas to climb at Tahquitz *before* going to Yosemite. Every spring even the native climbers spend a week at Tahquitz getting in shape for the Valley walls.

■ **Artificial Climbing.** Because most piton cracks are vertical and there are few ceilings, the double-rope technique, standard throughout the rest of the world, is never used in Yosemite. Nor is tension used except on overhanging rock. Instead, only one rope is run through all of the pitons and large numbers of runners are used to eliminate rope drag. The use of one rope has greatly increased the efficiency, simplicity and speed of artificial climbing.

■ Stirrups (slings) made of 1-inch-wide nylon webbing have taken the place of step stirrups. There are many reasons for this: 1. The slings grip the sides and cleats of the climbers' heelless *kletterschuhe* and give a much greater feeling of security and comfort, especially when belaying in slings for a long period of time. 2. The slings can be used for runners around large blocks, bushes or trees. 3. In an emergency they can be cut up and used for rappel

A pendulum traverse on the original El Capitan Nose route.

Modern Yosemite Climbing

Rappelling down a cliff is one of the simplest climbing techniques to learn. Yet it is one in which the climber depends fully on his equipment, unlike upward climbing, in which a safety system is in reserve. The majority of fatal accidents in Yosemite climbing have happened during rappels.

Outer Limits, a recent free climb, being led without pitons. Nuts (artificial chockstones) have replaced pitons on most of the commonly repeated routes in Yosemite, and where they cannot be used, pitons or expansion bolts are left in place for later parties.

slings. 4. They can be carried more neatly on the person or pack. 5. They can be used for prusiking more efficiently. The only additional things needed are three small loops of ¼-inch or ⁵/₁₆-inch cord. 6. They make no noise so that the belayer can hear the little familiar sounds that help him to understand, without looking up, what the leader is doing and to anticipate the belay signals. 7. They allow one to "sit" in one's slings, thus saving a great deal of energy. 8. There is less chance of dropping them either when a piton pulls out or through carelessness. As far as I can tell, they have no disadvantages over step stirrups. Possibly the reason why they have not been adopted by Europeans is that they are unable to obtain the flat nylon webbing needed for their construction.

■ Each climber carries three 3-step slings. The leader never leaves them in place but moves them up from piton to piton. A carabiner is kept on each sling and is never removed. On low-angle rock, only one sling is used; on steeper rock, two are used, one foot placed in each. On overhanging rock, a third sling is used to clip into the next piton. When cleaning out a pitch, two or even three slings are often clipped together to reach pitons that are far apart.

■ The actual technique is done thus: A piton is placed, a carabiner is clipped in, the rope is inserted, and finally the slings are clipped onto this carabiner. On doubtful pitons, the slings are clipped in *before* the rope is inserted; the climber steps up and tests the piton and *then* inserts the rope. This leaves less slack in the rope if the piton should pull out. Of course, a carabiner must be used whose gate can still be opened while the carabiner supports body weight.

■ **Equipment.** The first pitons were developed for use in the Dolomites in limestone, where a piton is expected to flow into a very irregular crack or hole and fill all the tiny internal pits and irregularities and have such great holding power that it can never be taken out. It was generally considered that only a piton of very malleable steel or iron had the qualities to fulfill these requirements. All European pitons today are still being made thus whether they are going to be used in limestone or not.

■ John Salathé was the first to realize the need of a piton for climbing on granite. During his attempts on the Lost Arrow, he saw that he needed a stiffer, tougher piton that could be driven into solid veins of rotten granite without buckling, that was lighter than an iron piton, that had greater holding power, and that yet could be taken out faster and more easily and be used over and over again. Out of old Model A Ford axles, he forged some beautiful horizontals, which to this day are almost revered by those lucky enough to own them.

■ The alloy-steel piton is based on a theory radically different from that of the iron piton. It is not expected to follow cracks but rather to act like a spring, pressing against the sides. It has been proven to have greater holding power in granite and similar rock because it can be driven harder and deeper without buckling into the typical smooth cracks so that it is actually tighter. The entire length of the piton is stiff, so that the head does not bend when removed, thus making it possible to do a several-day, 300-piton climb without leaving a single piton in place. The invention of the alloy-steel piton is as important to rock climbing as is the new ice screw to ice climbing.

Modern Yosemite Climbing

■ In the early 1950s a new piton was invented by another famous Yosemite climber, Charles Wilts, which helped as much as anything to set such a high standard of artificial climbing. This piton, with a blade the size of a postage stamp, was appropriately called the "knife blade". It was the first piton to be made of chrome-molybdenum aircraft steel and could be used in very thin cracks where no other piton could possibly enter. Although they were originally made for artificial climbing, it was soon found that these pins often had even greater holding power than angle pitons. Gerry Gallwas in 1957 forged some regular horizontals out of chrome-molybdenum steel (SAE 4130) for the 1957 ascent of Half Dome; some of these have been used over a hundred times and are still in use.

■ Yosemite, as any granitic area, has many wide piton cracks. Wooden wedges were never much used because these large cracks are usually filled with dirt. Several persons made large angle pitons, some up to 4-inch-wide, of various materials. Some, made by William Feuerer for the 1958 ascent of El Capitan, were fashioned from aluminum channel, angle iron and cut-off stove legs.

■ All of these pitons were made by individuals in home workshops and available only to personal friends. Salathé sold a few, but most climbers thought his price of $.55 too expensive! In 1958 the author started to make this newer type of equipment on a commercial basis. He developed a new aluminum carabiner, stronger than existing steel models, which had a gate that could still be opened under a climber's weight and shaped to be used in combination with the Bedayn carabiner in the Yosemite method of artificial climbing. Ringless alloy-steel angle pitons were invented that were superior in every way to existing models. The larger angle pitons were made of heat-treated alloy aluminum to save weight. A full line of horizontals of alloy-steel was developed, ranging from a knife blade to a wedge.

■ Abortive attempts on Kat Pinnacle's west face showed the need for a piton which would go into tiny bottoming cracks* which even knife blades failed to enter. From the need came the "RURP". This "Realized Ultimate Reality Piton" helped to usher in the A5 climbing and was instrumental in allowing tens of existing bolts to be passed up and chopped out. These diminutive pins are far from being just novelties but have become an absolute necessity on nearly all of the newer climbs.

■ The importance of this new equipment can best be emphasized by saying that since 1958 every major rock climb in North America has used my equipment. The future of rock-climbing equipment lies in the use of the lighter steel and aluminum alloys. Weight is now the major problem to be overcome.

■ **Ethics and Philosophies.** The most obvious split between European and Yosemite rock-climbing philosophies is whether to leave pitons in or not. In Europe they are left in place. In Yosemite, even if a climb has been done a hundred times, the pitons are still removed. I believe that nearly everyone, whether European or American, agrees that if practical, a route should not remain pitoned. It is entirely practical in Yosemite to take the pitons out. With the pitons removed and with no guidebook to show the way, a third or succeeding ascent of a route is as difficult as was the second. It is conceivable that a climber who is capable of doing the Bonatti Pillar on the Petit Dru with all the pitons in might not be able to climb the north face of

* A crack where the piton hits bottom before being fully inserted.

Phil Gleason makes an attempt to climb a flaring chimney. In the
picture at the top of page 95 he falls. His last piton was about ten
feet below, and with the slack and stretch in the rope he fell 30 feet
before the rope caught him.

Phil Gleason at the beginning of a 30-foot fall (see page 94). He suffered only superficial scratches and scrambled up to give the climb another go. The picture was made with a telephoto lens from the ground.

Liebacking is an efficient but strenuous and scary method of climbing offset cracks.

Chimney climbing is claustrophobic, slow and relatively secure.
Yosemite lacks the large holds for face climbing found in many
other parts of the country, and often chimneys are the most
efficient way up the blocky cliffs.

Modern Yosemite Climbing

Half Dome, although both climbs unpitoned are of equal difficulty.

■ In the Alps climbing is not called artificial until a stirrup is used. Free climbing in California means that artificial aid of *any* sort is not used, whether it be a sling around a knob of rock, a piton for a handhold, foothold or to rest on. After a piton is placed for safety, it may not be used for aid in climbing without changing the classification of the climb.

■ Especially on short climbs, free climbing is forced to its limits. Guidebooks list not only the first ascents of a route but also the first free ascent. Some climbers feel that it is more of an honor to do the first *free* ascent than the actual first.

■ Nowhere else, except on the sandstone climbs of the Southwest, is the need for expansion bolts more pronounced than in the Valley. However, this does not mean that they have been indiscriminately used. Climbers have gone to extremes to avoid placing one of them, except for an anchor, where the ethics are less stringent. The usual attitude toward bolts is that they should only be carried by the better climbers because only they know when a bolt *must* be placed. If a bolt is put in and a later party feels it unnecessary, then it is chopped out. Lack of equipment, foul weather or a less-than-expert leader is never an excuse for a bolt.

■ It has become popular in other parts of North America, especially in the Northwest, to lay fixed ropes up a climb to avoid having to bivouac or take a chance with the weather. These ropes create an umbilical cord from man to where he truly belongs and to where he can quickly retreat if things get tough. This manifests American love of security and shows that the climber should not be there in the first place. The only routes now being done with fixed ropes in Yosemite are those that take so long on the first ascent that they could not be done in any other way; such are the multi-day routes on El Capitan.

■ Perhaps I have given the reader the impression that I feel that Yosemite is the only place to climb and that its philosophies and ethics are the last word. Personally, I would rather climb in the high mountains. I have always abhorred the tremendous heat, the dirt-filled cracks, the ant-covered foul-smelling trees and bushes which cover the cliffs, the filth and noise of Camp 4 (the climbers' campground) and worst of all, the multitudes of tourists which abound during the weekends and summer months. Out of the nearly 300 routes in the Valley, there are less than 50 which I should care to do or repeat. The climbing as a whole is not very esthetic or enjoyable; it is merely difficult. During the last couple of years there has been in the air an aura of unfriendliness and competition between climbers, leaving a bitter taste in the mouth. Like every disease, it was initially spread by a few, and now it has reached a point where practically no one is blameless.

■ The native climbers are a proud bunch of individuals; they are proud of their valley and its climbs and standards. An outsider is not welcomed and accepted until he proves that he is equal to the better climbs and climbers. He is constantly on trial to prove himself. When he is climbing, he is closely watched to see that he does a free pitch free, that he does not place more than the required number of pitons in an artificial pitch, and that he does the climb speedily. Climbers have left the Valley saying that they will never return because of the way they were treated by the native climbers. These problems will, in time, resolve themselves as the Yosemite climbers move

97

afield and see that there is no room or need for competition or enmity in the mountains.

■ There have been times when I have felt ashamed to be a Yosemite climber, and there are times when I feel as if I truly hate the place; but then there are times when I should rather be there than anywhere else in the world. If at times I hate the place, it is probably because I love it so. It is a strange, passionate love that I feel for this Valley. More than just a climbing area, it is a way of life.

■ **The Future of Yosemite Climbing.** Nearly all of the great classical lines in Yosemite have been ascended. All of the faces have been climbed by at least one route. This does not mean that there are no new routes left, because there are countless new lines on the cliffs which lie between the great formations. Some will be as difficult as any yet done, but that is all they will be. They will offer very little esthetic pleasure. The rock is often poor, the cliffs covered with bushes, and the cracks filled with dirt and moss; blank areas will require bolts. As a line becomes less logical and direct, the esthetic beauty of the climbing also diminishes.

■ To do a winter climb for the sake of making the first winter ascent is senseless. Winter conditions can be better than in the summer. To do a route under actual winter conditions means climbing immediately after a storm, which is nearly impossible and suicidal. Because the rock is so smooth, ice will not adhere to it except during and directly after a storm. To climb then means having to clear off all the *verglas* on the holds because the ice is too thin and badly anchored to climb on directly. To clean off all the *verglas* is a slow process. At Yosemite's low altitude, the hot California sun early in the morning loosens great sheets of ice and sends them crashing down.

■ Solo climbing will not be practical until the routes are pitoned. Otherwise, because of the great amounts of direct aid, a two-man party can climb faster and more efficiently on the big climbs. I doubt that the big walls will be pitoned for a long time to come. Besides, at present solo climbing is against the law.

■ Climbing for speed records will probably become more popular, a mania which has just begun. Climbers climb not just to see how fast and efficiently they can do it, but far worse, to see how much faster and more efficient they are than a party which did the same climb a few days before. The climb becomes secondary, no more important than a racetrack. Man is pitted against man.

■ The future of Yosemite climbing lies not in Yosemite, but in using the new techniques in the great granite ranges of the world. A certain number of great ascents have already been done in other areas as a direct result of Yosemite climbers and techniques, notably the north face of Mount Conness in the Sierra Nevada, the west face of the South Tower of Howser Spire in the Bugaboos, the two routes on the Diamond on Longs Peak in Colorado, the Totem Pole and Spider Rock in Arizona, the north face of East Temple in the Wind Rivers, the northwest corner of the Petit Dru (voie Américaine) and the first American ascent of the Walker Spur of the Grandes Jorasses in the French Alps. Although these ascents are as fine and as difficult as any in their respective areas, they are merely the beginning of a totally new school of American climbing, that is to say technical climbing under Alpine conditions.

A climber ascends a fixed rope during an unproductive attempt on a new El Capitan route.

Placing a piton for protection on the first ascent of a short free climb. This route is now done entirely on artificial chocks.

Walking back to camp after a multiday climb.

The opportunities here are limitless. I have personally seen in the Wind River Range and Bugaboos untouched walls that are as difficult and as beautiful as any ever done in the history of Alpinism. There are in the Wind Rivers alone opportunities for fifty Grade VI climbs. The western faces of the Howser Spires in the Bugaboos are from 3000 to 5000 feet high. The Coast Ranges, the Logan Mountains, the innumerable ranges of Alaska, the Andes, the Baltoro Himalaya all have walls which defy the imagination.

■ Who will make the first ascents of these breath-taking rock faces? From the Americas the climbers can come only from Yosemite. The way it now is, no one can climb enough in the high mountains to get in shape to do a Grade VI climb, either in the mountains or in Yosemite. These extraordinary climbs will be done by dedicated climbers who are in superb mental and physical condition from climbing all year round; who are used to climbing on granite, doing much artificial climbing and putting in and taking out their own pitons; who are familiar with the problems of living for a long time on these walls, hauling up great loads, standing in slings, sleeping in hammocks for days at a time; and who have the desire and perseverance needed to withstand the intense suffering, which is a prerequisite for the creation of any great work of art. Yosemite Valley will, in the near future, be the training ground for a new generation of super-alpinists who will venture forth to the high mountains of the world to do the most esthetic and difficult walls on the face of the earth.

Royal Robbins sits at a Camp 4 table with the assortment of gear for the second ascent of the El Capitan Nose in 1959.

CAMP 4

DOUG ROBINSON

[*Yosemite climbing has produced little journalism. People involved in the climbing scene have written mainly about big climbs in which they participated. The reason this book does not contain any articles on short climbs is simply that none have been written worth publishing. Mountain is a British magazine with a small American distribution. In July 1969 it ran a special issue on Yosemite. Part of that issue was this article on Camp 4. It is the kind of article that would never have been written without a request from a far-away publication whose readership was interested in, but unfamiliar with, Yosemite climbing. Written in the climber's vernacular—talus, carabiners, one-and-a-half-inch angles—it captures the image of living in Camp 4 in the Sixties.*]—G.A.R.

■ CAMP 4 is the physical and spiritual home of the Yosemite climbers. It lies near the geographical centre of the Valley, where the old and stable talus, long since grown over with oaks and lichen, comes down from under the north wall to merge into the river-bottom meadows. It sits under a canopy of oak and pine. In spite of the spectacular setting, it has become the most trampled and dusty, probably the noisiest, and certainly the least habitable of all Yosemite's campgrounds. It is the only camp kept open all year, and was for many years the catch-all for pets, trailers, and other hard-to-classify and vaguely undesirable Yosemite visitors. Yet the Yosemite climbers will stay nowhere else.

■ By day, and in midsummer, it is 'home' for tourist families, with their barking dogs and self-contained camping trailers complete with television sets. Towards evening, however, as the dust is being shaken from the last unwilling child before supper, the clanking horde begins to return. In twos and threes, talking and laughing—or with exaggerated weariness, set off by little sweat-etched lines on dusty foreheads—with their hands polished to a shiny slate color by carabiners, and with yet another fifty-cent pair of Granny Grundie pants hanging in tattered ribbons from their belts, they come to reclaim their campground. For, whether the tourists realize it or not, it is the climbers' campground. The campers have penetrated unaware into a magic circle; they stand undazed at the focus of a force field of tradition and emotion.

■ The National Park Service provides tables, and the climbers furnish them—their only vestige of home—in their own manner: oilskin tablecloth, stove, box of pots and pans, kerosene lantern, the inevitable red cover of Roper's *A Climber's Guide to Yosemite Valley*, various talismans—an onyx rain god, a broken one-and-a-half inch angle—and perhaps a battery record player with a collection of Beethoven and the Rolling Stones. An assortment of Klettershoes and boots, in various stages of decay, stand in a line under the table. The camp is completed by a collection of ropes, hardware, and hauling bags, piled against a tree; a bear-proof cache hanging overhead, and an open-air bed of pine needles—a comfortable several-months home. At

103

Mark Powell, Bill "Dolt" Feuerer, and Warren Harding (L to R) after
an attempt on El Capitan in 1957.

peak season, in the spring and fall, almost half the campground is furnished
in this fashion.

■ The boulders strewn around the campground probably first attracted
climbers to Camp 4. Mostly small-hold face climbing and mantles, the
boulder problems are basically unsuitable as training for the abundance of
crack climbing on the walls. Yet they are quite popular; an hour of
bouldering, while dinner is cooking, is common. The boulders serve other
functions. They are a natural meeting place, where the lone climber can find
a partner for a climb the next day. Also, for some reason, bouldering brings
out the curiosity in tourist chicks who come around to watch, chat, and
perhaps get invited to a party—thus satisfying yet another perennial need of
the Valley climbers.

■ Camp 4 evenings follow an irregular cycle of quiet nights and parties. The
balmy evenings, a welcome by-product of the blistering hot days, banish any
thought of seeking shelter. The climbers live outdoors for months at a time,
and their parties are always held in the open air. There have, of course, been
the legendary ones—as on the twentieth anniversary ascent of the Lost
Arrow, when fourteen climbed the spire. They tyroleaned off, and were
joined by thirty others, for beer and Teton tea around a fire on the rim.
Parties are frequent, often spontaneous, and always unpredictable. By the
time a party really gets rolling, it is late enough for the tourists to complain
of noise—so the revelers must move out of camp or face the inevitable
ranger. I remember one such evening when I had gone to bed early. I
awoke to see a climber, carrying a lantern and loudly calling directions,
leading from the campground a ragged procession of figures clutching wine

104

bottles. Bringing up the rear of the long line, quieter and rather more sure-footed than the rest, were two figures in Smokey-the-Bear hats.

■ Half a mile away, across the waving-grass meadows, the Merced River swings a wide arc, leaving Sentinel Beach in the quiet water of its lee. High above, Sentinel Rock watches all that transpires here, seeing without comment the climb-watching, girl-watching, dozing, swimming, and reading with toes wiggling in the sand. And sometimes, at night, the moon edges over Sentinel to see—brown tanned and wet-slick in its light, unselfconscious at last—dancers naked in the river, while part-full bottles of red wine list at crazy angles in the sand.

■ And the quiet evenings: a shirtsleeved group around a table; mugs of tea; endless discussions—of climbs, climbers, philosophy, religion, any and all subjects—and silences. With the end of a thought trailing off into the lanternlight, the last of the transients shut up and gone to bed, the very darkness seems to take on a new dimension—a depth and silence that thickens before you until the night becomes palpable. The spiritual attachments, the feelings of home in this dusty campground and of companionship with one another, become almost visible for a few minutes at day's end, before we walk silently away to drop tired bodies on to pine needles in the dark . . . to wake a few hours later, shivering slightly under oakbranch moonshadows, and crawl into the sleeping bag.

■ Morning: the sun climbs late into this deep valley, but the morning light is already a promise of the day's heat. The climbers are up early—not by Alpine standards, but compared to the tourists—and for a little while an expectant calm, broken only by the low familiar roar of a Primus making morning tea, hangs over the campground. Ropes, hammer, and swami are laid out on the end of the table. The hardware is racked, and hangs from its sling on a nearby oak branch. In this expectant hour, the climber's thoughts have already left Camp 4 and moved up the walls to the chosen problem of the day.

Camp bear and climber's car.

THE SOUTH FACE OF MOUNT WATKINS

CHUCK PRATT

[Warren Harding used to jog up the Half Dome trail to keep in shape. It became a game for him. Once he timed himself beginning at 11 am on a 100° July morning, not taking a single drink on the hike—3 hours and 55 minutes for the 16-mile round trip with 10,000 feet of elevation change. He admitted to a ten minute rest on the top of Half Dome, during which he stared at the face of Mount Watkins and traced a route with his eyes. □ A few weeks later he organized Yvon Chouinard and Chuck Pratt into a three-man attempt on the wall. The climb was made in Alpine style. No fixed ropes were used. Water, rations and equipment were kept to a minimum. □ Chuck Pratt's account of the epic appeared in the 1965 American Alpine Journal. *If anything, he has underplayed the seriousness of being on a huge unclimbed wall in the July heat without enough water, with perhaps too few bolts to reach the summit and with little chance of retreat from high on the wall. Many climbers feel that this story, told like a folk tale in simple words and phrases, is the best and most accurate portrayal of a Yosemite climb.]—G.A.R.*

■ THE HISTORIC first ascent of Yosemite Valley's El Capitan in 1958 opened a new era in Yosemite climbing. In subsequent years, three additional routes, each over 2500 feet in height, were established on the great monolith. El Capitan's great height, the sustained nature of the climbing and the resulting logistical problems required that the first ascent of these routes be accomplished in stages, with the use of fixed ropes to facilitate a retreat to the valley floor. Since the initial ascent of El Capitan, eight ascents of the various routes have been made, and climbers involved in this latter-day pioneering have gained great confidence and experience in sustained, multi-day climbing. By the summer of 1964, with new improvements in hauling methods and equipment, the time seemed ripe for someone to attempt a first ascent of such a climb in a single, continuous effort.

■ One of the few walls that had remained unclimbed by the summer of 1964 and which afforded a challenge comparable to El Capitan was the south face of Mount Watkins. Rising 2800 feet above Tenaya Creek at the east end of Yosemite, Mount Watkins rivals in grandeur even nearby Half Dome. Despite the obvious and significant challenge presented by the face, the mention of Watkins seemed to produce only a certain apathy in the resident climbers of Camp 4. Though many of them, including me, speculated on who would climb it, yet few of us were moved into action. Then one pleasant July evening at Warren Harding's High Sierra camp on the shore of Lake Tenaya, when the wine and good fellowship were flowing in greater quantity than usual, Warren showed me a flattering photograph of the south face and invited me to join him. In a moment of spontaneous rashness I heartily agreed, and we enthusiastically shook hands, confident that the fate of Mount Watkins had been sealed.

■ Several days later we were strolling through Camp 4, two rash climbers looking for a third, having agreed that on this climb a three-man party was a fair compromise between mobility and safety. However, our recruiting was unrewarded. The experienced were not interested; those interested lacked the necessary experience. By evening we had resigned ourselves to a two-man party when Yvon Chouinard walked out of the darkness. He had ten days to spare and wondered if there were any interesting climbs planned.

■ Within the week, after a reconnaissance trip to study the face and plan a route, we were assembling food, climbing equipment and bivouac gear for a four-day attempt on the face. The three-mile approach to Mount Watkins began at Mirror Lake. As we unloaded packs at the parking lot, two young ladies approached us to ask if we were some of *THE* Yosemite climbers. Yvon modestly pleaded guilty and pointed out our destination. They asked if it were true that Yosemite climbers chafe their hands on the granite to enable them to friction up vertical walls. We assured them that the preposterous myth was true. Then, with perfect timing, Harding yanked a bottle of wine and a six-pack out of the car, explaining that these were our rations for four days. We left the incredulous young ladies wondering about the sanity and good judgment of Yosemite climbers. And so the legends grow.

■ After following the Sierra Loop Trail for two miles, we eventually began contouring the slopes above Tenaya Creek until we reached the base of Mount Watkins, where we sought out a suitable camping spot for the night. In the darkness we noted with apprehension that the granite bulk of Mount Watkins completely obliterated the northern quadrant of the sky. The following morning we awoke grim and significantly silent. With lowered eyes we approached the base of the wall.

■ Unlike most major Yosemite climbs, Mount Watkins has very little climbing history. Warren had been 700 feet up some years before, and climbers had studied the face from the southern rim of the valley, but ours would be the first and only all-out push for the summit. On his brief reconnaissance, Warren had been stopped by an 80-foot headwall above a large, tree-covered ledge. After studying the face three days before, we had elected to follow his route as it involved only third and fourth class climbing and would allow us to gain a great deal of altitude on the first day. By climbing a prominent corner at the left end of the tree-covered ledge, we could gain enough height to execute a series of pendulums in order to reach a comfortable-looking ledge at the top of the headwall, thus eliminating the necessity of bolting 80 feet. This ledge would then give us access to an 800-foot dihedral system on the right of the face. The dihedral eventually connected with a thin, curving arch leading westward across the face. We hoped this arch would take us to the great buttress in the center of the face and that the buttress would in turn take us the remaining 500 feet to the summit. However, these speculations would be resolved only after several days of sustained, technical climbing. The personal challenge, the unsuspected hardships, the uncertainty, in short, the unknown, which separates an adventure from the common-place, was the most appealing and

The South Face of Mount Watkins

stimulating aspect of the course of action to which we had committed ourselves.

■ Our immediate concern was transporting 100 pounds of food, water and equipment up to Warren's previous high point. Loading everything into two large packs, Warren and I struggled up the handlines left by Yvon as he led ahead of us up an intricate series of ledges and ramps. By noon we reached the tree-covered ledge and the base of the headwall where Warren had turned back before. Having volunteered to haul the first day, I began repacking our loads into three duffel bags while Warren and Yvon worked their way up the shallow corner at the left end of the ledge. Two free-climbing pitches brought them to a ledge where they investigated the problems of the long pendulums necessary to reach our goal for the first day—the comfortable-looking ledge 80 feet above me at the top of the headwall. By mid-afternoon Yvon had descended 75 feet, climbed across a delicate face and after trying for half an hour to place a piton, resigned himself to a bolt. Descending once more, Yvon began a series of spectacular swings trying to reach the ledge above the headwall. After numerous failures he finally succeeded by lunging for the ledge after a 60-foot swing across the face. Warren rappelled to Yvon and after dropping me a fixed rope joined him in an effort to reach the great dihedral which we hoped to follow for 400 feet.

■ Prusiking up the fixed rope, I could watch Yvon leading an overhanging jam-crack in the dihedral. From the ledge I began hauling all three bags together. I was using a hauling method developed by Royal Robbins for the El Capitan routes. It consisted of a hauling line which passed through a pulley at the hauler's anchor. By attaching a prusik knot or a mechanical prusik handle to the free end of the line it was possible for me to haul the loads by pushing down with my foot in a sling instead of hauling with my arms. The method was highly efficient and far less tiring than hauling hand-over-hand.

■ Yvon and Warren returned to the ledge after leaving 200 feet of fixed rope and we settled down for the first bivouac of the climb. After only one day on the wall it was evident to all of us that our greatest difficulty would be neither the climbing nor the logistics but the weather. It was the middle of July and temperatures in the Valley were consistently in the high nineties. We had allowed ourselves one and one-half quarts of water per day per person—the standard quantity for a sustained Yosemite climb. Still, we were not prepared for the intense, enervating heat in which we had found ourselves sweltering for an entire day. Those mountaineers who scorn Yosemite and its lack of Alpine climbing would find an interesting education by spending a few days on a long Valley climb in mid-summer. Cold temperatures and icy winds are not the only adverse kinds of weather.

■ The following morning Warren and I ascended the fixed ropes and continued climbing the great dihedral, hoping to reach its top by the end of the day. The climbing was both strenuous and difficult as we resorted more and more to thin horizontal pitons and knife-blades driven into shallow, rotten cracks. However, our biggest problem continued to be the heat. We were relieved only occasionally from the unbearable temperatures by a slight breeze. Although we tried to refrain from drinking water during the day so as to have at least a full quart each to sip at night, we were all constantly digging into the climbing packs for water bottles. Every few minutes we found it necessary to moisten our throats since even a few breaths of the dry, hot air aggravated our relentless thirst. Even the hauling, which should have been a simple task, became a major problem. Yvon, who was hauling that day, exhausted himself on every pitch, becoming increasingly tired as the day wore on.

■ In the early afternoon, we were surprised by the passing of a golden eagle across the face. Welcoming the chance for a brief respite, we ceased our labors and watched as the magnificent bird glided effortlessly high above us. Although he presented an inspiring sight, we hoped his nest would not lie on our route. In the days to come, this eagle would seem to make a ritual out of crossing the face, sometimes as often as three or four times a day, as though he were a silent guardian appointed to note the progress of the three intruders who labored so slowly through his realm of rock and sky.

■ By the end of the second day, we reached a group of ledges so large and comfortable that we named them the "Sheraton-Watkins." It was here that we were faced with the first major setback in our carefully planned route. The top of the dihedral was still some 200 feet above us. That 200 feet presented not only rotten, flaky rock and incipient cracks, but also the probability of having to place a large number of bolts. Now that we were within 200 feet of the prominent arch we had seen from the ground, we could see clearly that it did not connect with the large buttress in the center of the face, but that a gap of 100 feet or more separated them. The prospect of bolting across 100 feet of blank wall so appalled us that we began searching for other avenues of approach to the middle of the face. We were in a deep corner, the left wall of which presented messy but continuous cracks leading 80 feet to a ledge on the main wall. From this ledge, it appeared that a short lead would end on the first of a series of broken ramps sweeping westward across the face. It seemed the only reasonable alternative and we had just enough light left to ascend one pitch to the ledge 80 feet above before settling down on "Sheraton-Watkins."

■ We were up early the morning of the third day in order to accomplish as much as possible before the sun began its debilitating work. From our high point Yvon began the next lead. It was here that we began to literally walk out on a limb. We could see the broken ramps leading across the face for several hundred feet. Once we left the dihedral, retreat would become increasingly more difficult. Not only would the route beyond have to be possible, but we would have to consistently make the correct decision as to which route to follow. Using every rurp and knife-blade we had brought plus three bolts, Yvon succeeded in reaching the beginning of the first ramp. Then I began the first of three leads which were to carry us 300 feet across the face. Although the climbing was moderate fifth class, it required a great deal of effort. After nearly three days of climbing, the heat had reduced our strength and efficiency to the point where we moved at a snail's pace. Warren was barely able to manage the hauling bags without assistance and most of the afternoon was spent in getting our little expedition across the traverse. Although we had not gained much altitude, our efforts were finally rewarded when the traverse carried us into the buttress in the center of the face. Once again resorting to the indispensable rurps and knife-blades, I led a delicate and circuitous pitch past a dangerously loose flake to a curving

The South Face of Mount Watkins

arch. Following the arch as far as possible I descended, leaving what I thought would be a simple pendulum for tomorrow's climbing team. We were now situated on widely spread but comfortable ledges, and as we munched on our ever decreasing supply of cheese, salami and gorp, we caught a glimpse of our friend the eagle as he passed on his daily rounds.

■ At the end of this, the third day of climbing, we were well aware of our critical situation. We had brought enough water for four days. It was now obvious that we could not reach the summit in less than five. 700 feet remained between us and the giant ceiling at the lip of the summit and the route remained uncertain. We reluctantly agreed that it would be necessary to reduce our ration of water to provide enough for at least one additional day on the face. We did not yet consider the possibility of retreating although the prospect of facing the unbearable heat with less than an already inadequate supply of water filled us with dismay.

■ The fourth day proved to be one of the most difficult and uncertain any of us had ever spent on a climb. The sun continued its merciless torture as Yvon and Warren returned to the struggle. Warren found that I had

Chuck Pratt (L) and Yvon Chouinard in 1964.

"Warren had refused to take any water that day, preferring to give the climbing team every advantage."

underestimated the pendulum. After an agonizing effort, he finally succeeded in swinging to a ledge and I proceeded up to haul. By mid-afternoon, after climbing as slowly as turtles up the central buttress, we reached the most critical point of the climb. Above us a blank, 60-foot headwall topped by an overhang blocked further progress. Warren had nearly fainted several times from the heat, Yvon was speechless with fatigue and I was curled up in a semi-stupor trying to utilize a small patch of shade beneath an overhanging boulder. In an effort to provide more shade we stretched a bivouac hammock over our heads, but it provided little protection. For the first time we considered the possibility of retreating, but even that would require another day on the wall. It seemed that those very qualities which had made the climb so appealing might now prove to be our undoing. Warren investigated the possibility of rappelling 100 feet in order to reach the opposite corner of the buttress. However, we did not want to lose 100 feet of hard-earned altitude, especially since we could not be certain that the left side of the buttress continued to the summit. After a barely audible consultation, we decided to try the headwall above us, hoping eventually that we would find cracks leading to the summit, still 500 feet above us. Warren volunteered to go up first. After placing three bolts, he came down, too exhausted to continue. I went up next and with extreme difficulty placed two more, the first direct-aid bolts I had ever placed, barely adequate, even for aid. Yvon took my place and after breaking two drills was able to place one more before relinquishing the lead to Warren. Instead of placing more bolts, the latter lassoed a small tree and prusiked 15 feet to a horizontal crack. With a magnificent display of spirit and determination, Warren continued the lead over the headwall, did some extremely difficult free-climbing and reached a ledge adequate for a belay. Refreshed in spirit if not in body, Yvon followed the lead in semi-darkness, marvelling at Warren's endurance. Leaving a fixed rope, they returned and we all collapsed gratefully on barely adequate ledges.

■ By the fourth day Yvon had lost so much weight from dehydration that he could lower his climbing knickers without undoing a single button. For the first time in seven years I was able to remove a ring from my finger, and Harding, whose resemblance to the classical conception of Satan is legendary, took on an even more gaunt and sinister appearance.

■ We slept late the fifth morning and awoke somewhat refreshed. Confident that we would reach the summit by nightfall, we ascended the fixed rope to study the remaining 400 feet. Once again we were faced with a critical decision. Continuous cracks led to within 100 feet of the summit, but it appeared that they would involve nailing a long, detached flake. Yvon led an awkward pitch that curved to the left around a corner. After joining him, I dropped down and swung to the left corner of the buttress. Still I was unable to see if that corner of the buttress continued to the summit. I decided to climb the cracks above Yvon. They were of jam-crack width and I pushed the free-climbing to my limit in order to conserve the few bongs we had brought. After a fierce struggle through bushes I was able to set up a belay in slings. That morning we had had two full quarts of water for the three of us. Yvon and I had already finished one quart and when he joined me I was surprised to find he still had a full quart. Warren had refused to take any water that day, preferring to give the climbing team every advantage. His sacrifice was a display of courage and discipline that I had rarely seen equaled.

■ With added incentive, Yvon led a mixed pitch up a strenuous and rotten chimney, executing some gymnastics at its top to gain a narrow ledge. He joyfully announced that the next pitch appeared to be easy aid climbing and that the summit was only 200 feet above him. Anxious now for the top, I climbed as rapidly as I could while Warren struggled resolutely below with the bags. What we thought was a detached flake from below turned out to be a 100-foot column, split on either side by a perfect angle crack. The right-hand crack seemed to require fewer bongs so I quickly nailed my way to the column's top, a flat triangular ledge only 80 feet from the summit. It appeared that the next lead would just skirt the gigantic ceiling at the lip of the summit.

■ Yvon, resorting one last time to rurps and knife-blades, tapped his way to the crest of Mount Watkins just as the sun went down. His triumphant shout told me what we had all waited five days to hear. When Warren reached the ledge, he asked to clean the last pitch as he felt that he had not contributed enough that day! Warren Harding, who had been the original inspiration for the climb, whose determination had gotten us over the headwall below and who had sacrificed his ration of water after five days of intense thirst felt that he had not done enough! I passed him the rope and as he began cleaning the last pitch of the climb, I settled down on the ledge to my thoughts.

■ In the vanishing twilight, the valley of the Yosemite seemed to me more beautiful than I had ever seen it, more serene than I had ever known it before. For five days the south face of Mount Watkins had dominated each of our lives as only nature can dominate the lives of men. With the struggle over and our goal achieved I was conscious of an inner calm which I had experienced only on El Capitan. I thought of my incomparable friend Chouinard, and of our unique friendship, a friendship now shared with Warren, for we were united by a bond far stronger and more lasting than any we could find in the world below. I wondered what thoughts were passing through the minds of my companions during the final moments. My own thoughts rambled back through the entire history of Yosemite climbing—from that indomitable Scotsman Anderson, who first climbed Half Dome, to John Salathé, whose philosophy and climbing ethics have dominated Yosemite climbing for nearly twenty years, to Mark Powell, Salathé's successor, who showed us all that climbing can be a way of life and a basis for a philosophy. These men, like ourselves had come to the Valley of Light with a restless spirit and the desire to share an adventure with their comrades. We had come as strangers, full of apprehension and doubt. Having given all we had to the climb, we had been enriched by a physical and spiritual experience few men can know. Having accepted the hardships as a natural consequence of our endeavor, we were rewarded by a gift of victory and fulfillment for which we would be forever grateful. It was for this that each of us had come to Yosemite, and it was for this that we would return, season after season.

■ My reverie was interrupted by a shout from above and in the full, rich moonlight I prusiked to the top where Yvon was waiting for me. Warren had hiked to the summit cap to see if anyone had come to meet us. He returned alone and the three of us shared some of the happiest moments of our lives. As we turned away from the rim to hike to Snow Creek and some much-needed water, I caught a last glimpse of our eagle, below us for the first time. In the moonlight, he glided serenely across the face as majestic as always, and as undisturbed by our presence as he had been five days before.

THE NORTH AMERICA WALL

ROYAL ROBBINS

[In contrast to the clean whiteness of the southwest face of El Capitan, the rock on this route is dark and sometimes ugly. The climb is named after a map of North America crudely imprinted by Nature on the southeast face. This was the first El Capitan route on which no fixed ropes were used. A reconnaissance was made almost to the halfway point, but from higher on the overhanging route a retreat might not have been possible. For years this was considered the most technically difficult rock climb in the world. Recently, several new routes have been made on other parts of El Capitan which are at least as hard. Royal Robbins' account of the climb first appeared in the 1965 American Alpine Journal.*]—G.A.R.*

■ THE Sierra Nevada, a slice of the earth's crust 400 miles long and a hundred wide, was tilted upward along a fault line on its eastern edge. No cataclysm, this tilting took millions of years. When the range had attained nearly its present height, the Pleistocene epoch began, and with it a series of ice ages. During these periods of polar supremacy, glaciers flowed from the High Sierra toward the Pacific. In their ponderous descent they gouged a series of U-shaped canyons in the Sierra's western flank. Of these chasms, the one surpassing all others in sublime beauty is named after an indigenous Indian tribe: Yosemite Valley. If ever there existed an Eden, surely it was here. It is called "the Incomparable Valley," for the grace of the waterfalls, each with a distinctive personality; the diversified rock forms; the grand forests; the verdant meadows; and the moody, meandering Merced River.

■ Nothing contributes more to Yosemite's preeminent grandeur than a 3000-foot white monolith standing at the gate to the Valley: El Capitan. "The Captain" it indeed is, for it commands the attention and respect of everyone entering Yosemite. Its light igneous rock is called El Capitan granite. From the south to the west buttress, four great routes lie on this fine, hospitable granite. But the southeast face is different, for the granite is displaced in the center of that wall by brittle black diorite. This diorite forms a crude map of the North American continent, whence the name, "North America Wall."

■ Because of its grim aspect, this dark wall was left untouched while the more obvious and esthetic lines on the southwest face were climbed. But the inevitable attraction of a great unclimbed wall finally prevailed and in October of 1963, Glen Denny and I made several probes, reaching a high point of 600 feet. The aid-climbing was unusually difficult. Promising cracks proved barely usable. On the third pitch nearly every piton was tied off short.

■ In May, 1964 Tom Frost joined us in a major reconnaissance. He was a happy addition to our little team for reasons besides climbing talents, for

El Capitan in winter. The North America Wall is visible above the large tree on the right side.

The North America Wall

Tom has a large reservoir of that most important ingredient in alpinism: spirit. And despite his record in championship sailboat racing and his almost unrivalled list of great rock climbs, Tom is brazenly modest. This modesty combined with talent and cheerfulness make him an excellent climbing companion. On our reconnaissance Tom led the infamous third pitch in a way that made me wonder if it was as hard as I had originally found it.

■ In three days we climbed half the wall, reaching Big Sur Ledge, 1200 feet above the ground. Here the main problems would begin, but we had a good ledge to work from. On the fourth day, we rappelled to the ground, the lower four rappels being to and from anchors in a blank wall. As I prepared the last rappel, two tiny frogs crept from a crack and cavorted happily on my anchor pitons.

■ We planned to return in the autumn for an all-out effort to reach the summit, but left no fixed ropes. The era of siege climbing via fixed ropes is past in Yosemite. This era was inaugurated by Warren Harding on the south buttress of El Capitan. After this historic ascent, the siege technique was perhaps misused. At any rate, its passing is symbolized by the first ascent of the south face of Yosemite's Mount Watkins, done in one fine effort of five suffocatingly hot days. Harding was a member of the team. Likewise, we wished to do the North America Wall in as classical a style as possible. Siege climbing makes success certain, thus depriving alpinism of one of its most important elements: adventure. What fun is there in a game when the odds are a hundred to one in your favor?

■ We half expected (and half-hoped) others would do the climb before we returned. But when Tom and I arrived back in Yosemite the wall stood sombre and still virgin—waiting. In mid-October the Sierra was still in the

Yvon Chouinard (L) and Royal Robbins wait out a snow storm high on the North America Wall.

grip of an Indian summer. The Merced had lost its earlier vitality and become a trickle amid sand dunes. The evanescent Yosemite Falls, stupendous in June, had disappeared. The oaks and maples were slow to don their fall clothing; and each afternoon haze crept up the western foothills and filled the Valley—a rare occurrence in a normal autumn. I received a letter from Glen Denny saying he could not come. This was a great loss. We had already invited Chuck Pratt. Luckily, Yvon Chouinard was in the Valley. We persuaded him to join us.

■ We all felt similarly about the climb—it was not an appealing wall. It did not have the elegance or majesty of the southwest face. The treacherous dark rock, the difficulty of retreat due to great overhangs and long traverses, the absence of a natural route, and finally the apparent necessity for many bolts rendered us not happily enthusiastic about the venture. A large part of our individual selves did not want to attempt this face. But another part was lured on by the challenge of the greatest unclimbed rock wall in North America. Perhaps it would be a greater adventure for its ogreish appearance. But Chouinard forecast our doom. His previous bad luck on El Capitan had convinced him a black cloud hung over him.

■ We waited for the heat to abate. The southeast face is peculiarly a heat problem. Its concavity creates an oven sheltered from westerly breezes by the south buttress. Dwindling time forced us to start. In mid-afternoon of October 22, with sweat oozing from every pore, we carried supplies to the base of the wall. Tom and Yvon climbed the first pitch and left a rope on it. We then passed the night at the foot of the face. Yvon hardly slept.

■ Next morning, with the sun beating upon us, we climbed upward. As Tom led the second pitch, a tiny horn supporting an aid sling broke, causing a fall. His piton held and he passed the difficulty with a skyhook (a variously-sized hook used to support an aid sling from flakes, nubbins, and tiny ledges). Chouinard verified my opinion of the third pitch. He called it the hardest aid pitch of his experience. A short fall was held by a rurp (a tiny, slightly wedge-shaped piton, normally used only for aid).

■ Meanwhile, Chuck and I were hauling the party's 200 pounds of food, water and equipment. The heat was withering. Our 60 quarts of water, which gave us each one and a half quarts per day, would not be enough if this persisted.

■ We passed the night on long, narrow Mazatlan Ledge, 500 feet up. Next morning the circles around Yvon's eyes told of another sleepless night. After Chuck led past the cavernous overhang known as the Gulf of California, I pitoned and climbed familiar bolts (we had previously placed 19) to "Easy Street," a large broken ledge at 700 feet. We doggedly climbed without enthusiasm in the fierce heat, unconsciously saving ourselves for the forbidding problems above.

■ Arriving at our previous high point late on the fourth day, Tom

Chouinard does a rare move of free climbing on the black diorite of the North America Wall.

Chouinard jumars past a large ceiling, a long way out from the cliff.

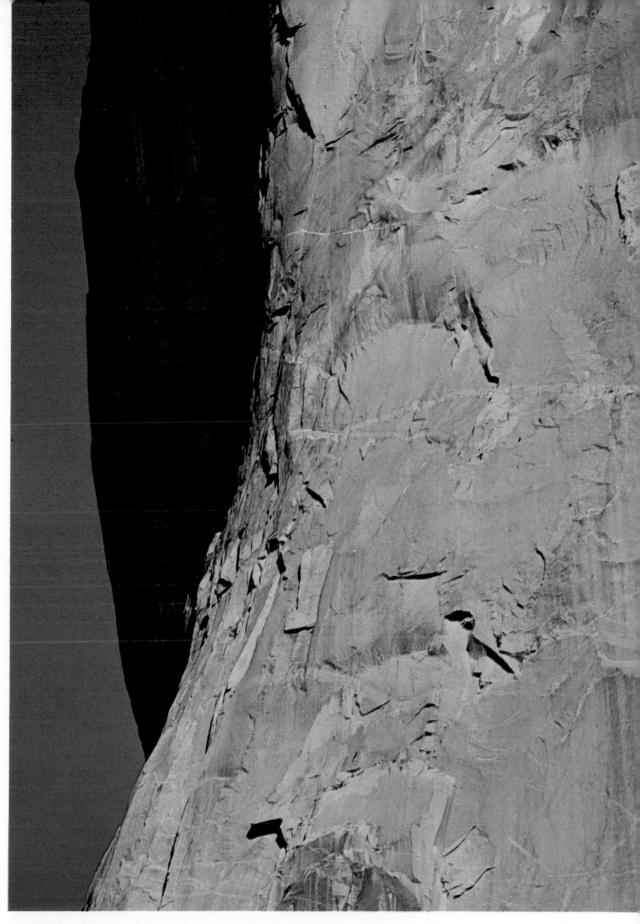

*A telephoto view of the midriff of El Capitan. A climber wearing red
can just be seen in the lower right-hand third of the photo making an
early and unsuccessful attempt to climb the Wall of the Morning Light.*

121

Fall colors, Bridalveil Fall and the Leaning Tower.

Dennis Hennek, Chuck Pratt and Royal Robbins on the Tis-sa-ack route on Half Dome.

Jim Bridwell on Flatus, a moderately hard free climb near Reed Pinnacle.

124

*Royal Robbins free climbing a traverse during the first ascent of the
North America Wall on El Capitan.*

Bivouac during the first ascent of the El Capitan Nose.

Chris Vandiver leads Outer Limits, a difficult free climb, using nuts for protection. Pitons are no longer being used on most of the popular climbs in Yosemite.

Sentinel Rock in midwinter. The west face is in the sun, the north wall in shadow.

continued, reaching a spot halfway across the 150-foot "Borderline Traverse." This involved a unique maneuver. Through a carabiner attached to a bolt sixty feet above, we lowered Tom to a point almost level with us, but thirty feet away. With a separate rope to his waist we pulled him toward us. When we had him tight as a stretched rubber band we let go, and he pendulumed far away. After several attempts he reached a flake otherwise inaccessible. He then proceeded upward by chipping the edge of the rickety flake and hanging aid slings on the small horns thus created. Finally a blank wall forced the reluctant placing of a bolt, and Tom returned to our ledge, happy with his fine work. Yvon began to sleep well.

■ On the fifth day Chuck and I completed the traverse across the light-colored granite and climbed 200 feet up the Black Dihedral, thus returning to the diorite and its consequent problems of pitonage and loose blocks. The return to Big Sur Ledge was made after dark. This night climbing, forced by short days, was to be a familiar pattern throughout the climb.

■ The tension we were all feeling was broken occasionally by gales of near hysterical laughter and jocose badinage:

"Hey, Yvon."

"Yeah, Chuck?"

"Say, you remember your nightmares, and I'll remember mine, and each morning we'll trade. OK?"

■ These two make a remarkable pair. They are both short, but Yvon is shorter. This gives Pratt the opportunity to take out his frustrations on someone smaller than he, and he rides poor Yvon mercilessly.

■ But what was Yvon doing on a nightmare-inducing wall like this? If there was ever anyone who has an eye for elegant routes on esthetic walls it is he. A poetic soul, Chouinard really rather disdains the analytical mind, for he hates to see beautiful things ripped and torn. He has the kind of mind which would make a good artist, but a poor chess player. Maddeningly creative, Chouinard has invented more techniques and devices in climbing than anyone I know. And here he was, stuck on the least esthetic great wall in the Valley with three El Capitan veterans; this would be his first El Capitan climb.

■ Pratt, on the other hand, had already climbed three great routes on El Capitan, though never one like this. Chuck's fantastic native talents and unassuming demeanor make him the finest of climbing companions; while his infinite patience and sense of humor make him an excellent teacher and guide. He enjoys severe climbs and easy ones, and will repeat a route many times if he likes it. Like Jack London and Thomas Wolfe, Pratt is an incorrigible romantic and suffers from the anguish which is a corollary of that *Weltanschauung*. Perhaps Chuck loves climbing partly because rock walls, unlike humans, are without malice.

■ The heat wave broke on the sixth day. We reluctantly left our cozy ledge and crossed the traverse to our high point. The section above was ugly. Overhanging to the right 400 feet, the Black Dihedral was a rotten mess. Dropped here by the leader were many rocks and huge balls of mud and grass. Luckily, these objects fell harmlessly far out to the side of us below. Chuck and I, doing the hauling that day, sometimes had to let ourselves out as much as fifty feet in order to prusik straight up to the end of a pitch. After dark, we reached the Black Cave, an alcove with no bottom. Here we spent

Belaying from slings near the start of the climb (4th pitch).

Royal Robbins hauls a pack across a horizontal traverse. Tom Frost led this section in a unique fashion. "With a separate rope to his waist we pulled him toward us. When we had him tight as a stretched rubber band we let go . . ."

Chuck Pratt profiled against the mottled
rock.

. . . and on a bivouac ledge enjoying a
drink and a rest.

several hours stringing our hammocks and getting settled. By flashlight Tom observed large centipedes crawling on the wall above.

■ At dawn, casually glancing over the sides of our hammocks, we were astonished at the tremendous exposure. The ground was 1600 feet straight below. Suspended over space, we hung one above another, like laundry between tenement flats. Oppressive is the word for the Black Cave. We felt we had climbed into a *cul de sac*. As we breakfasted on salami, cheese, and a mixture of candies and nuts, cirro-stratus began to cover the sky. My wife Elizabeth, through our tiny two-way radio, told us a storm was forecast.

■ Chuck led the overhang. He pitoned up one side of it and followed a horizontal dike of aplite around the top. Fascinated, we watched the lower part of Chuck's body move sideways thirty feet across our line of vision. Pitonage was very difficult, and Chuck's hauling line hung far out from the wall. When all cracks stopped, he ended the pitch and belayed in slings, thus finishing the most spectacular lead in American climbing.

■ I followed and was forced to leave two pitons because of awkward reaches.

"Man, that was really a fantastic lead. What exposure! Congratulations!"

"Thanks, Dad."

"I certainly don't want to go back down that overhang."

"Me neither. Looks like we might just reach the Cyclops Eye, if we go like hell."

■ We all started pushing as fast as safety would allow, for fear of a bivouac on a blank wall in a rainstorm. We climbed onward, searching, always searching. Searching for handholds and footholds, for piton cracks and the right piton. And searching ourselves for the necessary human qualities to make this climb possible. Searching for adventure, searching for ourselves, searching for situations which would call forth our total resources. For some it is a search for courage. Perhaps if we can learn to face the dangers of the mountains with equanimity, we can also learn to face with a calm spirit the chilling specter of inevitable death.

■ Rain had begun before we reached the shelter of the Cyclops Eye, well after dark. The Eye is a great hole in the rock, 200 feet high and 30 feet deep. We would be sheltered from the rain as long as the air was still. That evening, we were serenaded through our radio by our good friend Mort Hempel, singing rare and beautiful folk songs. As leaves are wafted by a breeze, so our spirits soared upward on the exquisite melodies of Mort's art.

■ The rain ceased next morning, but clouds persisted. The forecast was a three-day storm. We had already begun to ration food, so it would be a close contest.

■ Yvon led. He moved with cat-like grace which belied the difficulty of the free climbing up the loose flakes and shattered black rock. Then Tom nailed horizontally forty feet in a lead of exceptional severity. Late in the day Yvon led to the top of the Eye. This was the sort of pitch one never wants to do again, as it involved placing large angle pitons straight up between loose, overhanging blocks. The return to the bivouac ledge after dark was an exhaustingly slow and hazardous process.

■ While Chuck and I had been preparing the bivouac at dusk, menacing clouds, like sharks of various sizes racing after their prey, scudded toward us on a strong south wind. That night, the edge of a great storm moved east over California. Throughout central and northern California southerly gales swept the land, and the dry earth soaked up the downpours. As the storm rose to pass the Sierra, the rain turned to snow at 7000 feet. There we sat, in the furious, inky night, lashed by wind and rain, tiny mites tied to a great rock. Yet the rock itself was dwarfed by the majestic whirlpool of air moving out of the Pacific, and this same storm was just a small blotch on the earth's surface. The earth in turn would be a mere dot on the sun, and there are suns many thousands of times larger than that fiery orb giving us life. Mankind is truly insignificant. Man's fate, indeed, is to have to swallow these truths and still live on. If one could only find meaning to make these hard truths of insignificance and omnipresent death acceptable. Where to find this meaning? Again the search . . . and we climb on.

■ The storm abated in the morning and through the mist we perceived the Sierra had donned its winter coat of white. We were sodden. Tom especially had had a bad night. The previous day's climbing had been tough and Tom, always a big eater, was suffering from the stringent diet.

■ The new forecast was encouraging. The storm, instead of continuing eastward through California, had taken a northeastern tack and spared us several days of rain or snow. We climbed on through light showers that day, flabbergasted at the continuing challenges. A climb with such unrelenting difficulties was a new experience to us.

Yvon Chouinard on a traverse near the summit. El Cap Tower on the Nose Route is visible at the far left.

Frost, Robbins, Pratt and Chouinard (L to R) stand in a fresh foot of November snow on top of El Capitan after the North America Wall.

■ Above the Cyclops Eye I hand-traversed left from Chuck's hanging belay. Then my friend lowered me from a sling on a horn and I reached around a corner and started nailing upward beneath a curving arch. The crack was stubborn, accepting pitons grudgingly. I moved upward on rurps, knifeblades, and the tips of angles, slipping on the moss-covered rock, while ice water ran down arms and legs. At the top of the arch a sling through a hole in the flake and then a skyhook got me on my way hand-traversing left again. After twenty feet I was forced to stop and hurriedly place a piton. I then nailed straight left another twenty feet. The exposure was terrifying. At the end of the traverse I got a knifeblade piton behind a dubious flake. A skyhook on a tiny ledge got me five feet higher. Standing for twenty minutes in short slings I drilled a hole and placed a bolt, a poor one for it chipped away the rotten diorite. It was our 38th and last bolt. One hundred feet higher I reached the "Igloo," a sandy-floored cave 300 feet below the top. One of the hardest leads of my experience, it was just another pitch on this wall.

■ Next morning, nature smiled. The eastern sun, with beams of warmth, cut the crisp clean air, while the white panorama of the High Sierra, "the gentle wilderness," stretched from northeast to southeast, a deep blue sky arching above. Half Dome, as ever, stood sublime, a new cap of white on its bald head. We felt joyous to be greeted by such a magnificent morning. The beauty, the expectation of certain success, and the sun's heat made our blood race. All around us the exquisite splendor of these friendly mountains added to our elation. As John Harlin has said, "such beauty . . . turns satisfaction to pure joy."

■ Six hours later we had overcome the last problems and shook hands on top, happy as pagans.

Life in the tenement house of the Black Cave. From top to bottom: Frost, Robbins and Chouinard.

135

The Muir Wall ascends the blank-appearing area a few hundred feet left of the Nose Route. It begins in the middle of the picture and reaches the summit near the center of the right half in an obvious cleft.

MUIR WALL— EL CAPITAN

YVON CHOUINARD

[*After the North America Wall climb, Yvon Chouinard sought another increment of boldness. With TM Herbert he attempted to climb a previously unexplored route with just a two-man party. Battered by both rain and heat, they reached the summit with only one remaining bolt and no water.* □ *Readers will remember the large amount of equipment involved in the original ascent of the El Cap Nose in 1958. Chouinard and Herbert took the opposite approach; they planned the necessary goods down to the wire—and almost didn't make it. In the final days of the climb, they had pushed near their physical limit, and they began to experience the heightening of perception which comes before hallucinations. Chouinard touches on this ultra-awareness in this article, but a close friend of his, Doug Robinson, expanded upon it in an article entitled* The Climber as a Visionary, *first published in* Ascent, 1969. *Robinson wrote: "Chouinard's vision was no accident. It was the result of days of climbing. He was tempered by technical difficulties, pain, apprehension, dehydration, striving, the sensory desert, weariness, the gradual loss of self. It is a system. You need only copy the ingredients and commit yourself to them. They lead to the door. It is not necessary to attain to Chouinard's technical level—few can or do—only to his degree of commitment . . . Vision is intense seeing. Vision is seeing what is more deeply interfused, and following this process leads to a sense of ecology. It is an intuitive rather than a scientific ecology; it is John Muir's kind, starting not from generalizations for trees, rocks, air, but rather from that* tree with the goiter part way up the trunk, *from the rocks as Chouinard saw them, supremely sufficient and aloof, blazing away their perfect light, and from that air which blew clean and hot up off the eastern desert and carries lingering memories of snowfields on the Dana Plateau and miles of Tuolumne treetops as it pours over the rim of the valley on its way to the Pacific."*]—G.A.R.

Just beyond this glorious flood the El Capitan Rock, regarded by many as the most sublime feature of the valley, is seen through the pine groves, standing forward beyond the general line of the wall in most imposing grandeur, a type of permanence. It is 3300 feet high, a plain, severely simple, glacier-sculptured face of granite, the end of one of the most compact and enduring of the mountain ridges, unrivaled in height and breadth and flawless strength.
—John Muir, *The Yosemite*

■ MORE than any other mountain or formation, El Capitan has been responsible for the changing philosophy and the rising standards of American climbing. I speak not only of rock climbing but of ice as well, for new standards of ice climbing are being established by Yosemite-trained "rock specialists."

137

■ The new philosophy is characterized by small expeditions going into remote areas and trying new and extremely difficult routes with a minimum of equipment, no support parties nor fixed ropes to the ground; living for days and weeks at a time on the climb and leaving no signs of their presence behind. This purer form of climbing takes more of a complete effort, more personal adjustment, and involves more risk, but being more idealistic, the rewards are greater.

■ Probably the basis for this type of climbing was established by the naturalist John Muir. He used to roam the Sierra for weeks, eating only bread and whatever he could pick off the land, sleeping under boulders in only his old army overcoat, and rejoicing with the summer storms. He chose to accept nature as it was without trying to force himself onto the mountains but rather to live *with* them, to adjust *himself* to the rigors of this sort of life.

■ It was a vigorous life indeed, but his writings tell us of his communion with nature and his profound mystical experiences. Scientists will explain that when the body is weakened by fasting the senses become more acute and receptive. This partly explains Muir's mysticism but does not explain how, even though he was essentially fasting, he still managed to keep his prodigious strength. The answer to this is simple; he was fully adjusted to his environment and to eating less food.

■ This same attitude was later accepted by John Salathé and "Axe" Nelson, who trained their bodies to do with very little water in anticipation of their 1947 Lost Arrow climb. Their five-day ascent with only one pint of water per man per day is still the most remarkable achievement in American climbing.

■ The nine-day first ascent of the North America Wall in 1964 not only was the first one-push first ascent of an El Capitan climb, but a major breakthrough in other ways. We learned that our minds and bodies never stopped adjusting to the situation. We were able to live and work and sleep in comparative comfort in a vertical environment. When the food and water ran low, we found that we could obtain an enormous amount of energy from eating just ten raisins. We reached the summit feeling as if we could go on for another ten days. No longer would we ever be afraid of spending so many days on a climb, whether it was a Yosemite wall or a long Alaskan ridge.

■ After this climb we asked ourselves the inevitable question, "What next?" The answer was obvious . . . another first ascent on "El Cap" in one push with two men instead of four. This would not only double the work load and responsibility, but would also considerably decrease the safety factor.

■ It is the unknown that frightens brave men and there are plenty of unknown factors in trying a new route on this great wall. In the spring of 1965, after studying our proposed route for two years, calculating our equipment down to the last piton and cup of water, and weighing the consequences of a failure high up on the face, TM Herbert and I felt at last ready for the big push.

■ Our proposed line started to the left of the Salathé-Wall route, ascended some inside corners and arches, crossed the Mammoth terraces and continued more or less up, keeping to the left of the south face or "Nose" route.

■ **June 14:** In the cool early morning we walked to where we had left our duffel bags and equipment the day before. The climb begins at the "Moby

Climbing on "Moby Dick," a 200-foot practice climb at the base of El Capitan which is the beginning of the Muir Wall route.

Dick" slab, a popular two-pitch climb of F9 severity. From the ledge at the top we dropped down *en rappel* for twenty feet to the left and began nailing up. The pitons held well but they were awkward to place in the inside corner that leaned left. There was gardening of dirt and grass before a piton could be placed and as usual, belays in slings. We had to place two bolts in order to reach a sixty-foot-long horizontal flake and from these we hung our hammocks and had a secure, restful sleep.

■ **June 15:** I completed the traverse placing the pitons very carefully so that the flake would not expand. Then TM continued on, alternating pitons and bolts in a dangerous-looking loose arch. After reaching a trough-like groove, the climbing became easier and we rapidly gained height. Towards sundown TM pendulumed to a large ledge where we were to spend the night. Somehow our hauling system got fouled and many a terse word was exchanged and much needed water spent in perspiration before we were able to lift our two 50-pound bags onto the ledge. The strain of the climbing, the terrible California sun and that ever-present fear and uncertainty were all working away, and were reflected in us.

We had a fine ledge where we could lie out at full length and use our hauling bags for extra warmth. Besides, in the morning there would be no problem in having to repack the bags while hanging from pitons. The single fact that we had a ledge put us back into an elated mood and we joked and talked until we fell asleep.

■ **June 16:** As we had expected, the third day turned out to be mostly moderate free climbing up the right side of the "Heart." In the late afternoon we reached another fine ledge a pitch above the enormous "Mammoth terraces." The last lead was done in the rain as the weather had quickly turned from oppressive heat to a fine drizzle. When it began to pour in earnest we crouched in our *cagoules* and waited. In a brief break TM started nailing the next day's lead, while I belayed and collected water that was running down the rock. But the water had a bright green color and tasted so foul that we decided to keep it only as a reserve for the last day.

■ **June 17:** For the first half of the day we followed a single crack and then switched to another which we followed until we were forced to quit climbing early when the intermittent rain settled into a downpour. Since we were obviously in for a nasty bivouac, we prepared for it as best we could. We even tried to hang our hammocks above us as a shield against the torrents of rain. It never stopped all night and the cold was intense, as in a high mountain storm. Soaked through, we huddled together to keep warm. TM had a particularly bad night, shivering so violently that he could hardly speak. When he did, he sounded almost delirious. We were despondent and for the moment had lost the vision and our courage. Yet we kept any thoughts of retreat to ourselves.

■ **June 18:** The returning light restored our courage. A perfect crack in an overhanging corner allowed us to gain height rapidly while the overhanging wall shielded us from the rain. At the top of the corner Herbert began placing bolts across a blank area, doing a fantastic job of stretching out the distance between them. This traverse we hoped would lead us to the "Grey Bands" from where we would reach the beginning of the upper part of our route. After resting from the exhausting work of placing eleven bolts, all horizontally, he dropped down, went around a corner and began to layback up vertical flakes. Losing voice-contact with me, he painstakingly backed down until he could belay from the top of a very shaky flake. It was a tremendous effort and certainly saved the day. I just had time to finish the next pitch and to reach the "Grey Bands" before dark. We rappelled down to a good ledge and fumbled around in the dark to set up our bivouac. My down jacket was hopelessly soaked from the constant rain and so TM gave me his sweater, which had to do for the rest of the climb.

■ **June 19:** The cold grey dawn revealed an appalling sight. Barring us from the summit were 1000 feet of wild, overhanging wall capped by a 30-foot ceiling. A quick inventory showed two days' worth of food and water and only nine expansion bolts. There was no going down from here. The only practical retreat would be to traverse the "Grey Bands" for 400 feet to the "Nose Route", up which we knew we could make the top in two or two-and-a-half days. Aside from the uncertainty of the way ahead and our short supplies, we were physically and mentally exhausted from the strain of the climbing and the cold, wet bivouacs. Should we retreat or go on? Here was that line that has to be crossed of which Herzog speaks so eloquently in *Annapurna*. The cost of a failure can be dear, but the values to be gained from a success can be so marvelous as often to change a person's whole life.

■ After all, why were we here but to gain these personal values? Down below there were only ten people who even knew we were up here. Even if we were successful, there would be no crowds of hero worshippers, no newspaper reports. Thank goodness American climbing has not yet progressed to that sorry state.

■ Our decision made, TM led upwards. At this point the route becomes vague in my mind. The artificial climbing blends into the free. The corners, dihedrals, jam-cracks, bulges, are all indistinguishable parts of the great, overhanging wall. The pitches never end, and one day merges into another. I recall only bits and pieces. A horrible flaring chimney sticks in my mind, and the most difficult pendulum in my life. Always the overhangs and bulges keep us from knowing exactly where to go. And I remember a wonderful Peregrine falcon eyrie deep back in a chimney; soft white pieces of down stuck on to the crystals of grey granite.

■ **June 20:** The view below our hammocks was terrific—2500 feet between us and the ground. But that was another life and we began to discover our own world. We now felt at home. Bivouacking in hammocks was completely natural. Nothing felt strange about our vertical world. With the more receptive senses we now appreciated everything around us. Each individual crystal in the granite stood out in bold relief. The varied shapes of the clouds never ceased to attract our attention. For the first time we noticed tiny bugs that were all over the walls, so tiny they were barely noticeable. While belaying, I stared at one for 15 minutes, watching him move and admiring his brilliant red color.

■ How could one ever be bored with so many good things to see and feel! This unity with our joyous surroundings, this ultra-penetrating perception gave us a feeling of contentment that we had not had for years. It reminded TM of his childhood days when the family all came together on the porch of his home to sit and watch the setting sun.

■ The climbing continued to be extreme and in our now very weakened state strenuous pitches took us hours to lead. TM is normally a fairly

Royal Robbins nearing the top of the Muir Wall after his ten-day solo second ascent in 1968.

conservative climber, but now he was climbing brilliantly. He attacked the most difficult pitch of the climb, an overhanging series of loose flakes, with absolute confidence; he placed pitons behind the gigantic loose blocks that could break off at any moment, never hesitating and never doubting his ability.

■ **June 21:** Awakening on the eighth day, we promptly devoured the last few bites of food and the last of our water. Four bolts were left; 400 feet to go, and always that summit overhang weighing on our minds. It was going to be close. When the cracks were good, they were all one size; we had constantly to drop down and clean our own pitches in order to use the same pitons higher up. Often cracks were bottoming, which meant having to put pitons back to back and tying them off with only the tips holding. The slow progress was extremely frustrating. The rain continued to fall in a silvery

TM Herbert in rain garb during the first ascent of the Muir Wall.

curtain that stayed a good 25 feet away from us. Hanging from pitons under an overhang we placed our last bolt, hung by a "cliff hanger" on a tiny flake and barely reached a good crack to our left.

■ Our friends on top urged us on with promises of champagne, roast chicken, beer and fresh fruit. But the summit overhang still barred us and we almost insanely tried one blind crack after another. Finally, with the help of a light from above, we placed the last piton. We took a few halting steps on the horizontal and abandoned ourselves to a gastronomic orgy.

■ Looking back up at our route late one afternoon when a bluish haze covered the west side of El Capitan, it seemed to have lost a bit of its frightfulness but appeared even more aloof and mysterious than before. It is far too deep-rooted to be affected by the mere presence of man. But we had changed. We had absorbed some of its strength and serenity.

143

*"When Herbert isn't joking on a climb
you know he is scared."*
        –Royal Robbins

Muir Wall—El Capitan

Yvon Chouinard leading a difficult jam crack early on the Muir Wall.

Warren Harding on Half Dome. Clouds Rest in background.

146

RESCUE ON THE SOUTH FACE OF HALF DOME

GALEN ROWELL

[*In one very real sense the first multiday climbs were more bold and adventurous than the most difficult of modern routes. In 1947 Anton Nelson wrote the following words about his climb, with John Salathé, of the Lost Arrow Chimney: "We understood that rescue . . . in the Great Chimney was not to be expected." Today, a well-equipped rescue team of expert climbers can be dispatched by helicopter to almost any point in the Valley in a matter of hours. □ In the Sixties big-wall climbers realized that it would be only a matter of time before one of them was trapped high on a climb. Yvon Chouinard came very close three times in the span of one year. First on Mt. Watkins, when heat and lack of water almost took their toll; then on the North America Wall, when an October snow storm caught his party in a cave above an overhanging wall but relented long enough to let them reach the summit; and finally on the Muir Wall, when he finished an eight-day climb out of water and with only one remaining expansion bolt. Rescue from a big climb became an uncomfortable topic of conversation. □ In theory, rescue from a wall sounds like a simple affair: a big enough winch with a long enough cable should do the job. But someone has to get the end of the cable to the victims. They can't be hauled up like so much baggage. What happens if the cable or the person becomes jammed under an overhang? In practice, Yosemite rescues are being made with nylon ropes, rappels, Jumar ascenders and other items with which the climber is intimately familiar. □ In October 1968 two climbers were repeating a route on El Capitan. A storm came. Imagining their friends to be in trouble, a group of climbers organized a rescue with the aid of the National Park Service. Jim Madsen, a young climber who had done several routes on El Capitan, rappelled from the summit toward the storm-bound climbers. Somehow, Madsen fell out of his rappel and 3,000 feet to his death. The climbers, who had never requested the rescue, were suffering from exposure but still able to climb. The rescue was called off and they reached the summit under their own power. □ At the end of October 1968, only a few weeks after the Madsen tragedy, Warren Harding and I ventured onto the unclimbed south face of Half Dome. The face cannot be seen from any road or building, so we took small walkie-talkies with which to contact friends at planned intervals. What followed was the first successful rescue from the middle of a major Yosemite climb. Slightly different versions of this story appeared in* The Pitch, *December 1968 and* Summit, *May 1969. In July 1970 Warren Harding and I returned to the south face and made a successful but comparatively uneventful ascent.*]—G.A.R.

The Vertical World of Yosemite

> . . . the Dome . . . . would hardly be more "conquered" or spoiled
> should man be added to her list of visitors. His louder scream and heavier
> scrambling would not stir a line of her countenance.
> —John Muir, *The Yosemite*

■ I TURNED the page in the paperback and was deep in thought when a shout flinched me back to reality. It was Warren Harding's voice, calling for slack.

■ I was sitting in a belay seat as one or the other of us had been doing for almost six days now on this ledgeless wall. I reached for the Jumar, fed out four feet of slack, passed it around me and watched it disappear upward.

■ We were using a new belaying system in which the rope goes through a Jumar ascender after it runs around the belayer and through an extra carabiner hooked to the anchor. We were drilling our way up a blank section. For this type of slow climbing, the system has advantages. It frees the belayer's hands and affords the leader a safer belay than total reliance on a tired climber who may be daydreaming as he sits hours at a time.

■ I enjoyed daydreaming. The paperback discussed man's effect on Nature, and often a page would go unturned for half an hour as my thoughts wandered. I contemplated Huxley's likening of a human being on earth to a cancer cell on its host. Harmless by themselves, but endowed with the ability to reproduce until they destroy their matrix, the analogy was certainly well taken.

■ I contrasted Muir's thoughts of Half Dome's permanence with Huxley's of man's destruction of his environment. Had anyone ever contemplated that the development of climbing has paralleled the population explosion? Central Europe, host to the beginnings of mountaineering, was the first part of the world to feel overpopulation, soon lessened by migrations to the New World—which has taken up mountaineering rather recently, just as population pressure has begun to be felt. I searched for connections between the two. The climber's disdain for large groups of people, regimentation and technocracy seemed to bear this out. The mountains represent the stability and austerity of Nature in a world being raped by man. They are one of the few places where a man finds himself in competition with himself or his environment, not with other men.

■ It was this search for identity that placed us high on the 2,000-foot south face of Half Dome, little known to climbers or tourists. One's first impression is of a vast, curving slope quite devoid of features. A closer look shows an overhanging arch, leading halfway up the wall, and the realization that the wall is curved only on the edges. For the most part it is very steep (75°) and devoid of ledges or cracks.

■ We had reached the top of the arch in three days, arriving at a hauling bag hanging under an overhang from our previous attempt in 1966. Although torn and housing a swift's nest, it had contained three gallons of drinkable water and some canned food. From this point the route leads out of the arch by way of the most spectacular sixth-class lead I have seen. It nails horizontally for 10 pitons and then nails the convergence of two very overhanging walls for 10 more pitons. Warren called it his most strenuous lead. At the top of the arch the overhangs that we had been nailing consistently for three days ended and we climbed on a vast, open expanse of blank-appearing wall, stretching over a thousand feet to the summit.

148

■ The prospect of bolting a thousand feet of blank wall had stopped other climbers from considering the route. Studying the face through binoculars in winter and by blown-up photos, Warren and I found several disconnected crack systems. We decided that a route was possible with no more than 25 percent bolting. To make this 25 percent easier and faster, Warren developed a system of alternating bolts with rows of ground-down cliff-hangers placed in shallow drilled holes. Christened "Bat hooks," they saved about half the time of regular bolts, allowing us to cover about two pitches per day on the upper headwall. Free climbing, sometimes possible on the rough and lumpy sections, accounted for possibly 20 percent of our progress.

■ Now we were more than 400 feet above the arch with Warren leading. He had nailed an incipient crack for about 10 pitons and then begun drilling the blank rock above. He placed eight Bat hooks in a row before placing another bolt. After more Bat hooks he reached the end of the rope and tied into his last two bolts. I came up, and as I started the next lead we heard a shouted signal from our support party to turn on our walkie-talkie. We made contact with Glen Denny, assuring him all was well and three more days would get us to the top. He gave us a five-day forecast for cloudy skies but no storms, and said that he would go to the top by the trail and rappel on 750 feet of rope to take pictures. Warren signed off and I continued climbing toward one of several potholes on the face.

■ From a distance these potholes appeared as black specks against the white granite. Through binoculars they resembled shadowy caves. We joked before the climb that these were secret entrances to a giant room in the heart of the dome in which all the gods of the ancients lived. Warren's resemblance to Satan had often been noted. We half expected to be greeted at the doorway by a two-headed Janus who would calmly say, "Come in Warren, we have been expecting you."

■ Alas, the pothole did not hold such great things in store for us. It was merely a depression of dark rotten rock, perhaps five feet deep with no level place to even stand, much less sleep. Instead of a floor, it had a ramp inclined at almost fifty degrees. About 15 feet wide, it offered protection from the winds and was a more pleasant place to bivouac than on the stark face. I anchored with several pitons, hauled up the bags and prepared for the night.

■ Below, the clouds were putting on a grand show. Thinking of how John Muir might describe such a scene, I began to see things in a strange light. Muir was the first to recognize the importance of ice in forming Yosemite's features. Below me were two classic examples of glacier-carved mountains, Mt. Broderick and Liberty Cap. Toward the Valley they present sheer facades, but toward the high country, the source of the ice, they present shiny, smooth, mottled contours like those of giant lumpy balloons. Called "roches moutonnees" or sheep's backs by geologists, they are caused by grinding and polishing of the glacier that overrode them.

■ As I watched the panorama at sunset, I seemed to be riding backward in time. From the southwest came billowing cumulus clouds moving high and fast in the sky—colored orange and red in the setting sun. From the northwest came mare's tails, a form of cirrus clouds distorted by the winds, seemingly intersecting their brothers from the southwest directly above us.

Harding near the top of the 900-foot arch.

150

Galen Rowell approaches the lip of the arch, where the route follows the convergence of two overhanging walls.

Harding preparing for a bivouac on the smooth upper headwall.

But from the west came creeping, seething white clouds. They were so low that we couldn't see them until they came around the corner at the end of the Valley. The pure white veil slowly climbed the Merced River canyon and flowed between and around the sides of Mt. Broderick and Liberty Cap, just as the ice must have done in the opposite direction thousands of years ago.

■ The sound of Vernal and Nevada falls, which lie in the canyon just below the two mountains, had always been a subtle comfort to us. Otherwise, we rarely heard sounds unless we made them. The voices of the falls had become as familiar as our own. Nevada's low rumble. Vernal's higher-pitched roar, punctuated by slapping crashes when the wind changed the point of the water's impact. Now as the mist flowed in, they faded. As the sound deadened, the falls seemed farther and farther away. The formless cloud slowly rose, and soon Broderick and Liberty Cap were two bald islands in a sea of white mist below us. When it became dark, we closed ourselves in our special tent-hammocks. The mist gradually enclosed us in the night.

■ The hammocks were designed by Warren and were certainly the best yet for their purpose. They had a waterproof nylon cover that zipped shut to keep out wind and rain. The underside was heavy material with sewn straps running crosswise every few inches, converging on top in a single anchor point, instead of the two widely separated points of the usual garden-style hammock. This meant they could be hung anywhere instead of hunting for a spot where two anchors could be placed many feet apart. Even so, eight hours of continuous sleep was just not possible. Every hour or so we would wake with a pain from pressing against the rock, or with circulation cut off, or from a cold wind blowing upward against the bottom of the hammock.

■ Waking at midnight, I heard a new sound outside. It was the running of water and dripping of raindrops upon our hammocks. I went back to sleep, not worried because the weather forecast carried no prediction of a storm and therefore this must be a local disturbance. But several hours later, I realized my down footsack and jacket were soaking up water. The "waterproof" hammocks had been tested hanging free from a tree in the city, but not leaning against a rock wall running with water. The tightly woven fabric let water soak in, but would not let it out. Pools formed at the bottom of the hammocks. We had to puncture holes to let the water out. By dawn we were both soaked to the skin. Snow covered all the mountains in the high country. The rain became sleet and then turned into snow.

■ We had seen a practical demonstration of the forces that form the potholes. Ours was a focal point for the drainage from the upper face. We were in a small waterfall.

■ There was no chance of climbing in the cold, wet conditions. Besides, we believed that the local disturbance would move on and the sun would come out to dry us before the end of the day. After a few hours we heard a distant shout and turned on our radio. Glen asked how we were and said that he would not be able to rope down from the top today but he would tomorrow when the weather was better. We said that we were all right but very wet and cold; if things continued this way we would probably give up the climb and come up the rope he strung from the top. He said that was fine and he would see us tomorrow. He never did.

■ The weather became worse and worse. The snow fell thicker and thicker. Incredibly, it stuck to the almost vertical face and we were soon plastered. All day we shook with cold and looked for a blue spot somewhere in the sky. It never came.

■ We passed a second night in the storm. A sleepless, cold, wet ordeal. Fourteen hours of November darkness.

■ When the light finally came, everything was white. Small powder snow avalanches began to batter us about in our pothole. We were shaking almost uncontrollably and our fingers and toes were numb. Every article of our clothing was soaked and I was sure I could not last one more day and night. This was our eighth day and our second in the storm.

■ Zipped in my dripping prison I closed my eyes and imagined myself at home with my wife, two children and German Shepherd dog. It was Sunday morning. On most Sunday mornings I stayed in bed late. Then I would loll around the heater in the hallway and reluctantly drag myself to the breakfast table for food and hot tea. What I wouldn't give for a cup of hot tea!

■ I realized there was no chance of Glen climbing the cables. They were surely iced and in the path of frequent avalanches from the fresh snow hanging on the steep, featureless slabs. I tried to convince Warren that we should rappel down the route. He patently refused to have anything to do with rappelling. He said it was folly and he was staying where he was. I thought it was our only hope. Warren's refusal to move put me in a dilemma. I did not want to separate, which is against most ethics of climbing, but I did not want to hang in one place and freeze to death, as I thought we might after another night in the storm. Dying without an effort to escape seemed a most unforgiveable thing.

■ Slowly I climbed out of the hammock and began to set up a rappel alone. I would probably be forced to place several bolts as I would not always be able to rappel to piton cracks or bolts we had placed. Warren insisted on staying. I said that I would go down to the Valley and contact the park rangers to send a helicopter to rescue him. He said okay and I started down alone.

■ My immediate goal was the anchor bolt at the end of Warren's last lead, eighty feet below and thirty feet to the left. I hoped to go down, swing over to the bolt, anchor in, pull down the ropes and continue the descent. I got down the eighty feet, but because of ice on both the wall and my shoes, I could not move even two feet off the vertical track of the rope. My hands were numb, even in gloves. I realized my plan to descend was futile and decided to go back up. I clipped my Jumar ascenders on the rappel rope and put my weight on one. It slipped. I tried the other one. It slipped. The little teeth inside the gadgets were covered with ice and would not bite into the frozen rope. The two strands of the rope were both freezing to the wall and to each other. Even if I had reached the bolt, I never would have pulled down the rappel. The ascenders would not work at all. My strength was ebbing and I was aware that I might pay dearly for my rashness.

■ I was infinitely cold. My mind could not conceive of being colder. In mid-morning the face was letting loose much of its load from the night before. Small avalanches knocked me about as I tried to tie prusik loops with stiff hands. The prusik knots did hold my weight. They didn't slip down the rope. They froze in place each time I tightened one by putting weight on it. Very slowly I moved upward . . . stepping up . . . prying the frozen knot with my fingers out of gloves . . . releasing the knot and moving it up. After

153

an hour of repetition in agonizing slow motion, I was only halfway back to Warren. My hands felt like two boards. I often felt like blacking out and I had to make conscious efforts not to faint. Warren stood in slings at the pothole helplessly; there was nothing he could do. He couldn't help pull me up in these conditions any more than I could climb the rope hand-over-hand. I yelled at him to find all the slings he could, clip them together and lower them. They reached fifteen feet below him.

■ Life was now a line of gold rope stretching twenty-five feet to the bottom of the slings. My body revolted. It wanted to give up. My mind forced it to painfully and slowly move upwards . . . release a knot . . . move the knot up . . . release the chest loop knot . . . move it up . . . step up . . . etc. Finally I reached the slings almost two hours after I had started. I stepped into the lowest loop and quickly worked up to the pothole. Warren took off my pack. It was half filled with snow from the avalanches which had struck me as I was getting out the prusik handles and knots. He dug inside and got out my hammock. I quickly hung it up and got inside. I put my wooden hands between my legs and after a few minutes the agonizing pains of thawing began to shoot through me. I was now far colder and more miserable than before I had started the descent.

■ Just as I was warming up to the level of "very chilly" from that of "almost frozen," we heard a shout. Warren pulled a soggy looking walkie-talkie from the bag and miraculously it worked, although it was barely intelligible. Thank God! We came across clearly at the other end! Warren said: "We cannot last another night. Get us help today. A helicopter if possible. We are very, very cold."

■ They received us and answered that they would see what they could do. Meanwhile the storm was weakening. The ceiling lifted and the low clouds withdrew. Snow flurries became intermittent. About an hour later we were contacted again by radio and were barely able to make out words. After several repeats we finally got the message: "Helicopter . . . will . . . land . . . summit . . . two hours . . ."

■ It was now noon. The cold became more bearable. I began to smile and sing songs at the top of my lungs. We were saved. Waiting for a few hours was nothing like waiting the two days and nights we had already. Our ears were tuned for that special sound of a helicopter.

■ In less than two hours, Warren yelled "Here it comes!"

■ I listened . . . It was only a change in the voice of the waterfalls. Several times we thought we heard it, only to hear the falls go back to their normal voice. Finally at three o'clock we called back on the radio. I asked, "Where is the chopper?"

■ The reply was understood after many repeats: "Helicopter . . . coming . . . from . . . 200 . . . miles . . . here . . . before . . . five . . ."

■ I asked, "How will they rescue us?"

■ After more tedious repeats: "Will . . . drop . . . rope . . . to . . . you . . . anchor . . . summit . . . you . . . will . . . Jumar . . ."

■ I asked, "How will we know when the rope is anchored?"

■ The answer came: "We . . . will . . . tell . . . you . . ."

■ I asked, "It gets dark at five. What happens when it gets dark?"

■ We could not get a reply. Our unit had gone dead from water-logging. We waited in false anticipation, listening to what would sound like a

Harding peers from one of the fully enclosed hammocks he designed. Christened "Bat tents," these gadgets hang from a single anchor and permit a full night's sleep on a vertical wall.

helicopter but was only the fickle voice of Vernal Fall. Thousands of questions ran through our minds, unanswered. At four-thirty we heard a noise which became louder in logarithmic progression. Around the corner of the southwest face came the helicopter.

■ We smiled, waved and waited. It made lazy circles, gained altitude, flew near us and took off out of sight. Probably just checking the situation, we thought. Ten minutes later it came back, circling again and we saw it had a large spool dangling forty feet below it. We watched, expecting to see it drop the rope, fly toward us with the rope hanging and land on top. Again, it disappeared out of sight. We began to have grave doubts about the competence of the pilot. Twice more the chopper made passes near us. Then darkness came and the air was silent; helicopters do not fly in the mountains at night.

■ It certainly appeared that the pilot must not be experienced in mountain rescue work and could not figure a way to get us off. We were seven hundred feet below the summit, and on far too steep a face for him to fly very near.

■ We could think of dozens of grandiose rescue schemes. For instance, they could hover above the summit, drop a long rope to us, we would tie on, and then the helicopter would fly straight up like they do in the movies, land us on top, land itself, pick us up and tonight we would have a steak dinner in The Valley.

Rowell places a row of pitons to traverse under a long flake on the upper headwall.

Harding traverses under a severe overhang on the 900-foot arch.

156

Rescue on the South Face of Half Dome

■ Warren was the first to break illusions. He said that we might as well face up to the fact that we were going to spend another night on Half Dome whether we liked it or not. He was right. Well . . . sort of.

■ About an hour after dark I heard a strange noise, so I unzipped the hammock and saw a man being lowered on a rope not a hundred feet above us. Hope sent a pulsing warmth through our chilled bodies. I yelled up, "Are you one of the guys from that chopper?"

■ He was wearing a full down parka with a hood, carrying a walkie-talkie, a large pack and had a headlamp strapped to his forehead. From now on if I ever envision a guardian angel it will be in this form. I talked to the man on the rope for several minutes without recognizing him. Something about the voice, the mannerisms and the self-assuredness seemed familiar. Finally realizing who the rescuer was, I recalled an earlier scene, played on the same set, with two of the same players. Eleven years ago, the roles were transposed. Royal Robbins was coming over the top of the northwest face of Half Dome as his three-man party made the first ascent. Warren Harding was the only climber to hike to the summit to congratulate them. Now both the parts they played and the faces they climbed were reversed. Even after Royal reached us and I was talking to him, Warren didn't recognize him under all the paraphernalia. After several minutes, Warren leaned over in his slings, tried to look into Royal's face and said, "Who are you, anyway?"

■ After a good laugh, Royal acted like a true guardian angel, bringing us all our wishes. Besides bringing a lifeline to the summit, the depths of his pack concealed dry down parkas, gloves and even a thermos of hot soup. After putting on the parka and drinking my first hot liquid in eight days, I readied myself for Jumaring to the top. Royal had two extra pairs of Jumar ascenders and I clipped a set on the rope and started up. Only thing was I didn't move. The ascenders slipped, just as in the morning. In descending, the rope had rubbed the face and was now wet and icy. As I was getting discouraged Royal said that the higher I got, the dryer the rope. It was mainly wet on the bottom end from the vicinity of our pothole. I rubbed the ascenders up and down trying to make heat from friction to melt the ice in the little teeth. I fought my way fifty feet, rubbing the gadgets briskly on the rope and pushing the cams into the rope with my thumbs. Finally the slipping stopped. Less than an hour later I reached the top, where I was greeted by seven more people, including several good friends. I was ushered into a tent pitched in the foot of summit snow and given a swig of brandy, dry clothes and warm sleeping bag.

■ I realized that we had misjudged the rescue effort. Instead of checking the situation on each pass by the face, the pilot had been ferrying men and equipment from the Valley to the summit. They began immediate efforts to reach us in conjunction with our support party below the face, who also were given a Park Service walkie-talkie and helped direct Royal down to us in the moonlight on the half-mile-wide face. Since our radio was dead and we could not see the summit, we never knew what was happening.

■ Warren was right in a sense. We were spending another night on Half Dome, but not in the agony we expected. As he came up, Warren had more than his share of difficulties. He was wearing down-filled pants that had become waterlogged and then frozen. In order to start up the rope, he had to cut them in a few places to get sufficient movement in his legs. He had

157

The beginning of a storm on the south face.

also lost considerable weight through the ordeal. Lying in the tent we heard the following message come from Royal on the walkie-talkie: "Warren seems to be having a lot of trouble. His Jumars are slipping and his pants are falling off. He's really having problems!"

■ We didn't know then, but by some quirk of weather and radio waves, the entire rescue was broadcast through every television set in use in Yosemite, no matter what channel was tuned in. The picture was untouched, but the sound was from the walkie-talkies—loud and clear! The next day every Park employee with a television—and many tourists—knew about the rescue and the problems with Warren's pants.

■ By midnight everyone was on top and we spent a comfortable night on the summit. We ate canned fire-fighter's rations, which tasted to us like filet mignon. Early the next morning the sound of the helicopter came again. It landed on top, its blade spewing powder snow in a wide circle. Warren and I went down on the first shuttle. Are climbers scared of heights? Well, not usually, but I must admit that when the helicopter took off over the two thousand foot face, my heart was in my stomach.

■ We asked the pilot to fly by our route. To our surprise the bright red hammocks looked like pinheads on a distant wall as he flew by. When the helicopter neared the Valley floor, our thoughts turned to hot showers, hearty meals and walking, sleeping and feeling like normal men again—men who owe a debt to the prompt, decisive action of the National Park Service, the members of our support party and the climbers who selflessly performed the mechanics of the rescue. If we ever go back and finish the climb, it will surely be an anti-climax to the attempt preceding it.

The rescue helicopter on the summit of Half Dome. Nine men and their equipment were placed on the summit after numerous flights.

Yosemite Valley after the first fall snowstorm.

TIS-SA-ACK

ROYAL ROBBINS

[*There are four routes on the northwest face of Half Dome. Royal Robbins made the first ascent of every one of them. The most recent and difficult of the four is Tis-sa-ack, named from the Indian legend concerning the black streaks on the sheer face of Half Dome. This article, which first appeared in the 1970 issue of* Ascent, *was a major departure in writing style for Robbins. Instead of concentrating on his personal experience, he tried to picture the climb differently through the eyes of each person involved. Is it just Tis-sa-ack? Or has Robbins opened a can of worms that existed on other major climbs? For the first time, Yosemite climbers are presented as normal people who whine, complain and swear. We can only wonder if the strong, silent, square-jawed heroes of earlier Yosemite climbs are mostly fiction.*]—*G.A.R.*

■ **Hennek:** It was Robbins' idea, mainly. It was on a lot of guys' minds. Had been for a long time. I had thought of it, and when I loaned him my glass I figured he was taking a look. Meant more to him than anyone. He already had two routes on the face, and couldn't bear to see anyone else get this one. He wanted to own Half Dome.

■ **Robbins:** In the afternoon Marshall—I call him Marshall because Roper started that. Roper likes to call people by their middle names, and such. Like he calls me "Roy," because he hates the pretentiousness of my first name. And I can't help that. Anyway he likes to call Pratt Marshall, so I will try it for a while. Marshall led a nice pitch up into this huge slanting dihedral of white rock streaked with black lichen: the Zebra. Those black streaks, legend tells us, were made by the tears of the Indian girl for whom I named the route.

■ **Pratt:** I belayed in slings at the top of this pitch which wasn't too bad, except at the start where you're thirty feet out with nothing in and then you start aiding with a couple of shitty pins. Royal liked the next pitch because it was loose and gave him an excuse to play around with those damn nuts and feel like they were really doing some good, which I doubt. But I am, it's true, rather conservative. Then we came down on fixed ropes and slept on a big ledge we called the Dormitory.

■ **Hennek:** We would have been all right in the Zebra but we didn't have enough big pitons, even though we were carrying two sets of hardware. We needed about ten two-inch and a dozen inch-and-a-half pitons. The reason we had two sets of hardware is so one guy could be climbing all the time while another was cleaning. I led to the top of the Zebra and Pratt came up and started leading around the overhang at the top while Robbins cleaned the last pitch.

■ **Robbins:** From Hennek's hanging belay the crack widened to five inches. So Marshall used a four-inch piton, our biggest, endwise. It was weird, driven straight up like that. Then he got in a couple of good pins and used two nuts behind a terrible flake. Pitons would have torn it off. He didn't like it. Marshall hates nuts. He was talking about how it was shifting and then

lodging again, just barely. I think he wanted it to come out so he could say, Robbins I told you so. But it held long enough for him to place a bolt, but it wasn't very good because he wanted to get off that nut before the nut got off the flake.

■ **Hennek:** We couldn't see Chuck bolting above the overhang, but Glen Denny, who was taking pictures from across the way, got some good shots of us hanging there and Pratt working away. About dusk I lowered Royal out to jumar up and then I started cleaning the pitch.

■ **Robbins:** When I got up there I saw Marshall had managed to bash three pins into unlikely cracks. There was nothing to stand on. When I pictured the three of us hanging from those pitons I immediately got out the drill. Marshall isn't known as an anti-bolt fanatic—it's true about that thing on Shiprock, but that was mainly Roper—he isn't known as a fanatic, but there is no one slower on the bolt gun draw than Marshall Pratt. I got in a good solid bolt and we settled down for the night.

■ **Hennek:** Royal says settled down, but he didn't get settled very fast. He was screwing around and cursing in the blackness, and then I heard this rip. He had put too much weight in one end of his hammock, and he ought to know better having designed the mothers, and then there was this explosion of screeching and shouting and terrible foul language that would have done credit even to Steve Roper. I thought it was funny. It went on and on. Fulminations in the darkness. I was amazed that he so completely lost control because he always seemed like such an iceberg.

■ **Robbins:** I had a unique experience the next day: placing sixteen bolts in a row. It was just blank and there was no way around. But it was a route worth bolting for, and after a time I began to take an almost perverse joy in it, or at least in doing a good job. I put them in all the way, so they're good solid reliable bolts, and I put them quite far apart, so I think that it's perhaps the most craftsmanlike ladder of that many bolts in the world. Still, I was really happy to reach with the aid of a skyhook a crack descending from a ledge fifty feet higher. When Marshall came up he was raving. He raved a lot on that wall. He's an outstanding ravist, often shouting at the top of his lungs like Othello in heat. "Why, why, why," he shrieked, "Why didn't I re-up?" "Christ, I could be a sergeant by now, with security and self-respect. Why did I start climbing in the first place? Shit, I could have been a physicist, with a big desk and a secretary. A secretary!" he repeated, brightening, a leer breaking across his face. "But, no, no, I couldn't do that. I had to drop out of college. Because I . . . I," his voice rising in a crescendo, "I, like Christian Bonington, chose to climb." I was convulsed. We were having a good time. Nobody uptight. No ego trips. But we were low on bolts and low on water. We would have to go down the next day. It was late afternoon and. . . .

■ **Hennek:** I'll take over here to save all of us from another of Royal's glowing descriptions of how the sun goes down. After a night on the ledge—and a rather long October night at that—we rappeled, placing bolts and dropping from one hanging stance to another. We all wanted to return. It was going to be a good route and we left a lot of hardware at the base, to save carrying it up next time.

■ **Pratt:** But when next time came, in June, the summit snowfield was still draining down the face. It had been a heavy winter. So we put it off until the

163

fall and I went to the Tetons, Robbins went to Alaska to stroke his alpine
hang-up, and Dennis went fun-climbing in Tuolumne Meadows and
re-damaged an old injury so he was out of the running for the year. In
October I got a card from Robbins saying he'd be up in a few days for the
Dome, and when he didn't arrive it really pissed me off, and when days later
he still didn't arrive I said fuck it and made plans to go on El Cap with Tom
Bauman. Christ, when Robbins didn't show, people were looking for him on
Half Dome, solo. And then when he finally came up several days late his
mood really turned me off. He was tense and cold. He said he couldn't wait
until Tom and I had done our climb; he was taking the Dome too seriously,
so I decided not to go.

■ **Robbins:** When Chuck said he wouldn't go I was almost relieved. At least
now he couldn't make me feel like I was dirtying the pants of American
Mountaineering. I feel guilty with a camera when Pratt is on the rope. It's
like asking a Navajo to pose, and I would never do that. Marshall hates
cameras as much as he hates my puns and 5.10 psychos. He doesn't want
anything to get between him and the climbing experience. He suggested I
ask Don Peterson. Peterson had been up the Dihedral Wall and was hot to
go on anything as long as it was difficult. Although he had never studied the
wall, it didn't take much persuading.

■ **Peterson:** We agreed to go up in the morning. Robbins was like a man
possessed. He was totally zeroed in on Half Dome. He had a lecture date
soon and he had to squeeze it in. It rained like hell that night and looked
bad in the morning but Robbins figured we might as well go up because it
might not storm. I didn't like it but I didn't say anything and we started
walking up expecting to get bombed on any minute.

■ **Robbins:** Our loads were murderous. We stopped where the great slabs
begin and gazed upward. "Didn't know what you were getting into, did
you?" I asked, facetiously. "Well," replied Don, "it can't be any harder than
things I've already done." I turned absolutely frigid. The tone of the next
eight days was set right there.

■ **Peterson:** What I didn't like was his assumption of superiority. Like he
figured just because he was Royal Robbins he was the leader. I didn't buy
that. Christ, I had done climbs in the Valley as hard as he'd done, and I did
the Dihedral faster. Yet when we got up to the base of the wall he sent me
to fetch water. I just don't buy that crap.

■ **Robbins:** On the way up Don asked if there was anything on the North
America Wall harder than the third pitch. I told him no—as hard but not
really harder. Well then, he said, we shouldn't have trouble with the rest of
it. Mead Hargis and I have been up the third pitch and it wasn't too bad.
Oh, really, I said. Well, it might be a little easier now because Hennek and
Lauria had to place a bolt. Oh no, he said, we chopped it. We went right on
by. In a few hours we were at the Dormitory. It was strange climbing with
Don. Like many young climbers he was intensely impatient. He was used to
great speed and just going. Speed is where it's at. It's not the noblest thing
in climbing, but it moves many. Still, I didn't expect to feel the pressure of
Don's impatience running up the rope like a continually goading electric
current. And I didn't expect a generation gap, but there it was. For eight
days we would be locked in sullen conflict, each too arrogant to understand
the other's weaknesses.

Robbins leading overhangs on the lower part of Tis-sa-ack.

Don Peterson cleaning direct aid on Tis-sa-ack.

■ **Peterson:** On the second day we reached the top of the Zebra. Royal belayed in slings while I led the pitch over the top. Right away there was the wide crack. Robbins told me Pratt had knocked a four-incher endwise into the five-inch crack. I screwed around for a while, wondering why he hadn't brought a bigger bong this time. I couldn't get it to work so I took three bongs and put them one inside the other and that filled the crack okay, but God was it spooky. Still, I thought it was a pretty clever piece of engineering.

■ **Robbins:** After Don made this strange bong manoeuvre, he reached the flake where Marshall had had his wild time with those tiny wired nuts. "It's been a long time since I've used nuts," said Don, to cut the power of any criticism I might have of his chocking ability. After he had put his weight on the second one it pulled and he ripped out the other, falling fifteen feet. He didn't like that and this time he nested two pins first. But he still couldn't drive a pin higher as the flake was too loose so he put the nut back in and got on it. It was holding so he started to take in rope and as he was reaching for Pratt's bolt the chock came out and down he came, pulling the pins and falling twenty feet this time. I feared he might be daunted but he swarmed right back up the rope and got the top nut in and got on it and pulled in a lot of rope and got the bolt this time. Fighting spirit, I thought. I reflected how Don was a football player and how he must charge the line the way he charges up those pitches.

■ **Peterson:** Robbins was rather proud of his bolt ladder and bragged about it while he was leading it. I passed his belay in slings and led on up to the previous high point which Robbins called Twilight Ledge. In the morning he took a long time leading around several lips of rock. I was getting pretty antsy by the time he finished. Christ, was it all going to be like this?

■ **Robbins:** Above us rose a deceptive five-inch crack. Don went up to look at it and said do you want to try it? It won't hurt to try I replied, but when I got up there I wouldn't do it without a bolt, and we had no bolts to spare. So for about an hour I played with bongs driven lengthwise, and with four-inch bongs enlarged by one-inch angles driven across their spines. It was distasteful as hell, and if anything came out I'd be right in Don's lap. I was trembling with more than exertion when I finally clawed my way to Sunset Ledge. When Don came up I was gratified to hear him say he didn't think he could have done it. Maybe now the tension would be eased between us. He probably wanted me to say, "Sure you could," but I couldn't give up the one point I had won.

■ **Peterson:** It was a good ledge. We were halfway or more. It was my lead but Royal had a lot more bolting experience so he led off, placing a bolt ladder diagonally across a blank section. In the morning I finished the ladder, nailed a big loose flake and put in a bolt and belayed in slings. When Robbins came up three or four pins just fell out.

■ **Robbins:** The first thing I did was put in another bolt, for above Don's belay rose another of those vile five-inch cracks, too big for our pins and too small to get inside. I launched an all-out effort, struggling and thrashing desperately in the slightly overhanging crack. Four months later I still bear the scars. The top of the flake was like a big stone fence without mortar, but I got across that and placed a few bolts and then nailed a thin horizontal flake. I placed seven pins there and four fell out before I had finished. With

167

two good bolts for a belay and hanging bivouac I was safe and happy with nothing on my mind but the next 800 feet. Don wanted to try the jamcrack because I had said it was probably the hardest free climbing I had done on a big wall, but I told him we don't have time man, which we didn't. I was very relieved, for I was afraid he would come up easily and go down and tell the fellows I said it was hard but he didn't find it so. What the hell, that would happen in the next ascent anyway. Let the pitch have a reputation for a year.

■ **Peterson:** At about this point I wasn't feeling too happy. Robbins had taken almost a whole day to lead one pitch. I just didn't see how we could make it at this rate. I knew he had to place a lot of bolts, but it about drove me out of my skin waiting for him to finish. I felt I could have gone faster. We were using too many bolts when we still had this big blank section above us. What if we didn't have enough? But the only thing Robbins had to say was "We can always turn back, or else they can pull us off." I didn't think we were going to make it. I had never gone so slowly on a climb in my life.

■ **Robbins:** I hated drilling those bolts. We had these extra-long drills, that were all we could get at the last minute, and we had a long drill holder too, so I was bending over backwards drilling, and drilling is plenty bad enough without that. Here I was working away and always this mumbling and bitching from below, and finally the shocking ejaculation, "This is a lot of shit." From then on I felt I was battling two opponents, the wall and Peterson. I had learned to expect a grumble whenever I made the slightest error, such as not sending up the right pin ("Goddamn it, everything but what I need"), or forgetting the hauling line. I began to feel incompetent. It wasn't really so much what Don said, it was that he said it. It was a new experience climbing with someone who gave his emotions such complete freedom of expression. I was shocked and mildly terrified by Peterson's dark passions bubbling repeatedly to the surface. It probably would have been healthier to have responded in kind, to have shouted "Fuck you, Peterson," every time I felt scorn, real or imagined, coming my way. I didn't lack such feelings. The things I was calling Don were far worse than anything he said, direct or implied. But when I said them I kept my mouth shut.

■ **Peterson:** On the fifth morning I had to use up three more bolts because there was another five-inch overhanging crack. I finally got into it and went free for a hundred feet completely inside a huge flake for half the way. Then we had three straightforward pitches before some bolting brought us to a great ledge, where a ramp led up to a huge blank area below the summit. That night our water froze. In the morning I led up the ramp to a tight little alcove. The blank wall started about thirty feet up. It looked awfully big.

■ **Robbins:** As I nailed up to the blank area, I thought hard about our remaining thirty bolts. We would place some so they were barely adequate, allowing us to pull and re-use them. We had now traversed too much to descend. Those long drills were murder. I had three Rawl drills and another holder, and I used them to start the holes. They were extremely brittle, but I soon learned that a broken Rawl worked fine, and if they didn't break well, I would re-break them with the hammer. I was saving three short Star drills for the end. I didn't get far that day. It was slow going. I used one drill seven times before discarding it. Don spent the night scrunched in his cave while I bivouacked in a hammock. The weather, which had been threatening, was

Tis-sa-ack

holding well. The next day was an ordeal. Sometimes it took nearly an hour for one bolt. Whenever I wasn't drilling I had my head against the rock in despair and self-pity. And always that electricity along the rope, that distracting awareness that Peterson must be going mad. Poor Peterson, but poor me too. Besides the hard work, there's something mentally oppressive about being in the middle of a large, totally blank piece of rock. I was sorry I had disdained bat-hooks, believing as I had that if you're going to drill a hole you ought to fill it with a good bolt. I was so far gone now that anything went. I just wanted to get up. But there was nothing to do but what we were doing. When Don came up to my hanging belay the first thing he said was, "I was sitting down there for twenty-four hours!" That's energetic youth. Don had suffered as much sitting as I had drilling. That afternoon Don placed a few bolts, more quickly than I had, but with no more enthusiasm.

Chuck Pratt leads the first pitch of the Zebra during the first attempt on Tis-sa-ack.

The next day I again took over the bolting, inexorably working toward the barely visible lower corner of the dihedral leading to the summit overhangs. That edge of rock was our lodestone, drawing us like a magnet.

■ **Peterson:** Robbins had hoped to do the wall in six days, but this was the eighth. We really wanted to get off and thought maybe we could. The bolting was going a little faster now with Robbins using the short drills and not putting the bolts in very far. He would place one fairly well and then two poor ones and then another good one and then come down and take out the two bad ones and re-place them above. He did this about twenty times. Robbins rarely said anything while he was working on a pitch. He was like a beaver working away on a dam, slow and methodical. At times I felt I was going to burst, just sitting in one place doing nothing. I like to climb. This wasn't climbing, it was slogging. But I had to admire Robbins' self-control. He had about as much unmanageable emotion as an IBM machine.

■ **Robbins:** We reached our lodestone just as the sun was reaching us. Don eagerly grabbed the lead, nailing up from the last bolt. Thin nailing it was, too. By stretching a long way from a rurp, he drove a knifeblade straight up behind the rottenest flake imaginable. It seemed impossible it could have held. I had vowed that I wasn't going to give Peterson an inch, but I weakened. I told him it was a damn good lead. It would have been too flagrant not to have done so. We were now on a ledge beneath the final overhangs. Above, gently pivoting with grotesque finality in the afternoon breeze dangled a gangly form, mostly arms and legs, with a prophet's head of rusty beard and flowing locks. It was the artist, Glen Denny. He and the rock around him had already taken on a golden hue as I started up in an all-out effort to reach the top before dark. It didn't look far, but using two rurps just to get started was a bad omen. I went as fast as possible, but not fast enough to escape Peterson's urging to greater speed. The summit tiers overlapped one another, building higher and higher like the ninth wave. On several, reaching the crack separating the folds was barely possible. On one, a hook on the wire of a nut saved a bolt. Everything happened at once as I neared the top. The cracks became bad, the light went, pulling the rope was like a tug-of-war, and I was running out of pins. I had just gotten in a piton and clipped in when the one I was on popped. As I got onto the next one the piton below dropped out and then I was off the aid and on to a sloping smooth slab in the blackness, realizing I was really asking for it and picturing the fall and the pulled pins and hanging in space above Don. I backed down and got into my slings and cleaned the top pin with a pull, then began nailing sideways. Glen Denny is watching silently as I start to crack but I realize I am getting melodramatic and find myself looking at it through Glen's eyes, completely objectively and so cool down and feel with fingers the cracks in the darkness and bash away with the hammer smashing my fingers and pins coming out and me complaining in the darkness putting fear into the heart of my companion and asking him to send up his anchors so I can use them but he refusing and me saying to Glen that's the way it's been all the way up.

REFLECTIONS OF A BROKEN-DOWN CLIMBER

WARREN HARDING

[*The Wall of the Morning Light on El Capitan received more publicity than any other mountaineering accomplishment in American history. Even the American Everest Expedition did not get the coverage of this 27-day ascent by Warren Harding and Dean Caldwell. For the climbers it was instant public acclaim: TV talk shows, Wide World of Sports, lectures, offers from magazines and manufacturers. □ But the coin had another side. Among other climbers there was extreme resentment. Some felt that the route had been "forced" by using too many bolts up an "unnatural" line on El Capitan. Others thought the publicity was so extreme that it must have been rigged from the beginning. Twenty-seven days was regarded as just too long to spend on any rock climb; it was compared to flagpole-sitting. □ A few months after the climb, Royal Robbins made the second ascent in six days with Don Lauria in the middle of winter. An unusual tool was added to the normal selection of big-wall equipment: a cold chisel. Robbins' intention was to "erase" the route by removing all the bolts and other anchors left by the first party. After removing 40 of the 330 drilled anchors, Robbins stopped the bolt-chopping and continued the climb in a normal fashion. He explains his motives in the final chapter of this book. □ This article was written by Harding for the 1971 issue of Ascent. In contrast to Robbins, who is a frequent contributor to mountain periodicals, Harding had not published an account of any of his climbs for more than a decade, a rather novel situation for someone who was being taken to task for his "adroit use of the press". □ Harding freely admits that he and Caldwell hoped to get a little publicity. They had a friend who they asked to be liaison with the press, and they agreed not to release any information on the climb until it was well under way. On about the twelfth day of the climb their liaison man took to the Fresno Bee photographs that Caldwell had dropped from the route. He was turned down: "Who would be interested in yet another ascent of El Capitan?" For a while it appeared that Harding and Caldwell would not even be able to recoup food money from photos of the climb. Ironically, the mass publicity was generated by a rescue attempt which they neither requested nor accepted. As for the style of the climb, Harding gives his age-old answer. He simply wanted to climb the route and did it as best he knew how, in a single attempt without fixed ropes or prior reconnaissance. He placed drilled anchors where he thought they were necessary, following no one's dictates but his own. Many climbers disagree with Harding's concept of style. They feel that his joke about the climb being "an exercise in vertical freight-handling" proves that an excess of equipment came between him and his experience. But it is an experience that no one can take away.*]—G.A.R.

Warren Harding peers around a corner during an ascent of the
northwest face of Half Dome in 1964.

**"Climbing would be a great, truly wonderful thing if it weren't for
all that damn climbing."**

—John Ohrenschall

■ As I sit on the veranda of my quarters at TM Herbert's *Rock of Ages
Home for Old Climbers,* enjoying my Graham crackers and warm milk, I
think about the past 18 years . . . my rise and fall as a rock climber . . . what
a fine person I used to be . . . where did I go wrong?

■ Finally I realize what's wrong with me . . . why I'm rather oblivious to
many of the things around me. It's simply that I've spent too many nights
and days dangling from Yosemite's granite walls. My once keen analytical
mind has become so dulled by endless hours of baking in the hot sun,
thrashing about in tight chimneys, pulling at impossibly heavy loads, freezing
my ass off on long cold nights in various examples of the "ideal bivouac
gear," so that now my mental state is comparable to that of a Peruvian
Indian, well stoked on coca leaves. . . .

172

■ I've been at it too long . . . thought that when I'd cleverly run in front of a rapidly moving truck (Sept. '69) I'd be spared any further indignities (i.e., climbing). But my badly smashed right leg recovered sufficiently to allow me to pursue this ridiculous activity.

■ A couple of years ago I had met a rather unsavory character name of Dean "Wizard" Caldwell (Wizard?). As our acquaintance dragged on, I discovered that we had much in common. For one thing we were both rather lazy . . . an important quality of the serious climber. We talked much of past glories and future plans. But for the most part didn't actually do anything. Grandiosity of our plans seemed to be directly proportional to the amount of booze we would consume at a sitting. One night in the Mountain Room, completely taken by Demon Rum, we decided we would climb El Capitan's Wall of the Early Morning Light . . . The Big Motha' Climb!

■ We knew it was quite safe to indulge in such talk since neither of us was capable of climbing anything . . . . Dean had some badly torn ligaments, result of stumbling over a tree stump while walking to the potty room in Camp 12. My right leg was still pretty bad . . . weak knee would barely bend. Tried a new climb, east edge of Royal Arches, only got out about 40 feet. We adopted the name of "March of Dimes Climbing Team."

■ Fall—beginning to get worried now . . . physical condition has sufficiently improved; we can stall no longer. Began carrying loads up to the "base camp"; cloak of secrecy surrounding our activities . . . "great hairy giants" were all around waiting to annihilate any trespassers on "their route." Fearfully Wizard and Batso skulked around the valley. Difficult to be discreet carrying things like 12 gallons of water, big sacks of food, bivvy gear, 6 hauling bags and the like. Eventually got things sorted out and bagged up. Led and fixed the first two pitches.

■ Then, of course, the weather turned bad . . . sitting it out at Dave Hanna's place we were shocked to learn that the dreaded Royal Robbins had suddenly appeared in the valley . . . what now? Would he come charging up the wall . . . just plow us under? Desperately, we moved out.

■ Almost predictably, rain started falling as we reached the top of the first pitch where our five hauling bags were hanging . . . . So in mid-afternoon we set up our first bivouac . . . Bat tents with plastic tube tents over them. It soon became obvious that we had vastly underestimated the time that this venture would take us. Fortunately we had also greatly *overestimated* the amount of food and water required for a day's sustenance. We had figured 12 days stretchable to 15 days. (Turned out to be "stretchable" to 26 days).

■ End of second week . . . things looked different—very bad! We'd been on a rock wall longer than anybody else ever had (at least in Yosemite) . . . last two days in a wretched state of *soggification*. As the 15th day dragged on, still raining, we realized we were in a very critical position. We were only about halfway up . . . at the bottom of the Dihedrals, where our hopes of finding a good crack had come to nothing.

■ Our mental and physical condition had somewhat deteriorated from the effects of the soaking rainstorm, the general wear and tear of bashing our way up 1500 feet of the hardest climbing we'd ever experienced.

■ Dave Hanna and Pete Thompson came up to the base of the wall. . . . Bull-horn voices from below informed us that the weather forecast was not very encouraging: clearing tomorrow, but another storm on its way. . . .

■ We pondered the situation as the rain continued through the day and into the night. Realized it could take another 10 days to go the rest of the way. Carefully inventoried the rest of our remaining food. We'd have to radically reduce our rations if we were to stretch them out to even come close to finishing the climb.

■ But the thought of giving up the climb seemed simply unacceptable. It wasn't at all hard for us to make up our minds to press on . . . somehow try to make it. Another factor . . . the thought of trying to descend the 1500 feet of mostly overhanging wall with our gear made us retch!

■ Next morning we informed Dave and Pete of our decision to continue. They seemed to feel we were insane but. . . .

■ Weather cleared . . . a day to get dried out and reorganized, then come to grips with the Dihedrals. Only took us five days to get up this delightful area . . . lots of A4 nailing, bolting, riveting up overhanging bulges. On about the 20th day we heard unfamiliar shouts from below. The shouter identified himself as TM Herbert.

   "Hi TM—Good to see ya! What're you up to?"
   "We've come to rescue you!"
   " . . . . Whaaaaat?"

■ About this time Dean (leading) noticed ropes being lowered over the rim about 800 feet above. A great deal of shouting ensued. Most of our—uh—"rhetoric" would be unprintable in all but the most "advanced" periodicals. We did make it quite clear that we were fine, had the situation well in hand, were not about to be rescued. Fortunately those in charge of the rescue operation elected to suspend the effort, thereby sparing

"But suddenly it seems like a drag. Maybe I should have stuck with sports car driving."

El Capitan during the clearing of a storm when Harding and Caldwell were high on the face.

everyone some rather bizarre scenes: rescuers landing on Timothy Tower to find "exhausted" climbing team enjoying a fine mini-feast of salami, cheese, bread and an entire bottle of Cabernet Sauvignon (Christian Brothers, of course) all in a beautiful moon lit setting. Dialogue. "Good evening! What can we do for you?"

"We've come to rescue you!"

"Really? Come now, get hold of yourselves—have some wine. . . ." The action could have gone anywhere from there . . . a quiet intelligent conversation with the would-be rescue team returning in the morning via their fixed ropes. Or had the rescue team been over-zealous, a wild insane piton hammer fight might have followed. For we were very determined not to be hauled off our climb. We'd put too damn much into it to give up now! The hard part was behind us.

■ We were still feeling quite strong in spite of being on very slim rations for the past week. Perhaps our minds were becoming a bit fuzzy, though . . . had dark, cloudy visions of the National Park Service being influenced by envious, money-hungry climbers who would like nothing better than to fill their pockets with $$$ while removing two clowns from a climb they didn't deserve to be on. The wall would remain (with all the hard work done)

175

Reflections of a Broken-down Climber

Climbing by drill and hammer–the center of the controversy over Harding's climbs.

in a virginal state, awaiting a team of super climbers who could do it in real style. . . .

■ So onward and upward! . . .

■ Finally there was Dean battling his way up what we hoped would be the last pitch. But as he came to the end of the climbing rope, still about 60 feet below the rim, the day too came to an end! Frustrating—disappointing to be so near and yet have to wait until the next day, but no use taking a chance of blowing it now. . . .

■ Next morning I was totally unprepared for what I saw as I floundered up the last overhang onto the ledge at the rim . . . a veritable army of newsmen, friends, would-be rescuers (and a beautiful girl, Beryl Knauth). As I anchored myself to the ledge, I suddenly felt an overwhelming feeling of emotional release—sort of came "unglued" for a moment. Pulling myself together, I joined the happy carnival atmosphere that prevailed at the summit: batteries of camera snouts trained on us, gorging ourselves on all the food and champagne! All sorts of friends and well-wishers, ecstatic kisses and embraces—what a marvelous little orgy! Only thing lacking was a Mexican mariachi band!

■ But if I could have foreseen what would happen in the next few months I might have been tempted to say, "Oh, screw it all!" and bail off the top—well not really! With all the bullshit there were a lot of good things.

■ But there were ominous cluckings from certain pious experts about the degenerative effect on climbing of all the publicity attendant on such a climb. It would tend to attract hoards of unworthy persons to the rock walls and mountains—got to reserve all this for us "good guys." Keep the masses out! Maintain the esoteric image of climbing, raise the standards, etc., etc. . . .

■ It comes to mind that climbing is rather commercialized, certainly highly publicized, in Britain. Has this resulted in total deterioration of British climbers and climbing areas? It's my impression that it has not! Apparently Britain's relatively small climbing area is quite heavily used. Is the countryside becoming one huge garbage dump? I've been told by those who have been there that it definitely is not. Why? Could it be that the people, even though they are large in numbers, have come to know and love their mountains and desire to take care of them?

■ Elitists will argue that it is necessary to discourage the masses from mountain areas. No doubt this would work quite well in a feudal system where a small nobility had complete control of the peasantry. But such is not the case—theoretically, at least, this country operates as a democracy. . . . All, worthy or not, have equal right to the public lands. Again, theoretically, the use and preservation of our mountain areas would seem to depend on the vote of the masses. How, then, can we expect the support of the average citizen in conservation if he is told the mountains are too good for him, that they should be reserved for a minority of self-styled "good guys?"

■ Perhaps the hope of the "Valley Christians" lies in some form of regimentation patterned after the meticulous system of climber control so magnificently conceived and employed by the Soviets. Apparently well-structured training programs are carried out—screw-offs quickly weeded out!—examinations and ratings given, climbs assigned only to the properly qualified—everyone kept in his place!!

178

Harding in a comfortable bivouac beneath the Firefall Wall. The folding chair and cowboy hat were found on the ledge, apparently dropped by tourists from the railing directly above.

■ But this is digressing . . . back to what's important: climbing.

■ Why did we climb the Wall of the Early Morning Light as, how, and where we did? . . . I had always felt that the route should follow the right-leaning cracks in the lower section—traverse into the Dihedrals, then roughly straight up. This was not prompted by *Comician* ideals, but rather by some undefinable esthetic attraction this particular area held for me. As with some other routes—Leaning Tower, Half Dome South Face—I was not concerned about how many bolts it might take. It was simply that it appealed to me and I wanted very much to climb it!

■ With the storms—three in all—food shortage, and, most significant of all, the rescue fiasco, the whole thing, reflected by the press, captured the imagination of the public. Oddly enough, the "high adventure" magazines, *True, Argosy,* etc., showed only the mildest interest . . . maybe it was just a glorified flagpole-sitting exhibition after all.

■ But whatever it was (the real climbers knew!) there definitely was general interest. An exciting, fun-filled whirlwind tour of public appearances followed our return to the valley. Fame and fortune were ours!—though I did seem to be getting quite a bit more of one than the other; like my share of the proceeds—$1500 for four months' work. It didn't exactly seem like a "get rich quick" scheme. Anyway, at least there was great professional satisfaction: I had advanced from my lowly status of unemployed construction worker to the enviable position of unemployed TV star!

■ The emotional and monetary aspects of something like the aftermath of the Wall of the Early Morning Light are little short of amazing! Whether they like it or not, the principals involved suddenly become a business organization (or perhaps, a disorganization!). Some personalities can change significantly, others don't. Warm friendship and camaraderie can be replaced by cold contempt and suspicion. Happy laughter can turn to nervous, polite chuckles.

■ But we all know each other better now . . . for whatever that's worth. I

179

still believe that it's entirely possible to work with the various commercial aspects of climbing without destroying the flavor.

■ Do I really want to, though? What is this climbing trip all about, anyway? Does it really matter if a particular climb is done in any particular "style?" Is there one "true code of ethics" that is admirably suited to all climbers? There are those who profess to have the real answer. In other fields, so did Jesus Christ, Karl Marx and Adolf Hitler!

■ I have often been asked why I seldom, if ever, write my views on all this ethics business. In thinking about it, I realize I really don't give a damn. If all or most other climbers feel a need for the comfort and shelter of structured thinking—if there are those who feel a need to establish and promulgate these principles and lead the masses to a better 1984-ish life, fine with me! I still feel inclined to do my own thinking. As long as the V.C. don't get their own secret police and employ Spanish Inquisition methods, I won't worry about being imprisoned, stretched on a rack, forced to confess my sins, and then burned at the stake as a heretic. Rather, to the self-appointed Gurus, I say: Bugger off, baby, bugger off!!

■ As I observed earlier, I'm entirely fed up with all this crap about bolts, bat-hooks, press releases, commercialism, etc., etc. . . . At a trade show in Chicago, Dean and I received the electrifying news (rumor?) that R.R. and Don Lauria had just completed the second ascent of the Wall of the Early Morning Light, and had chopped out all the bolts and rivets; all this in only six days!!

■ Naturally many people at the show asked our reaction to this. At the time, the best we could come up with were weak little attempts at humor: "Oh, well—they're just faster than us. Chopping bolts? Whatever's fair, etc., etc."

■ But the questions still came, especially upon returning to Yosemite Valley.

A well-equipped tourist watches the progress of the Harding-Caldwell climb from El Capitan Meadow.

Harding during one of his many stormbound bivouacs.

■ "Well, Harding, how does this grab you? What do you think about the bolt chopping thing?" Frankly, I hardly knew what to say, or think. For one thing, it didn't seem worthwhile to go to all the trouble of finding out what had really happened. . . .

■ Still, some people thought that I should be concerned about all this—shocked, offended perhaps. Fact is, I don't give a rat's ass what Royal did with the route, or what he thought he accomplished by whatever it was he did. I guess my only interest in the matter would be the possibility of some clinical insight into the rather murky channels of R.R.'s mind.

■ Perhaps he is confusing climbing ethics with some fine (obscure?) point of prostitution morality . . . like, perhaps, a 100-bolt climb, e.g. Tis-sa-ack (or a $100-a-night call girl) is very proper; but a 300-bolt climb (or a $300-a-night call girl) is gross, immoral, or whatever. Or maybe Royal has gone the way of Carrie Nation—substituting hammer and chisel for hatchet! And then again, maybe it's got something to do with rivets—I don't know. In a way, I feel sorry for Royal (a veritable Alpine Elmer Gantry) with all these problems, bearing the responsibility of keeping rockclimbing the "heavy," complex thing it must be . . . (?)

■ Many years ago, when I first started climbing, it really seemed like fun. I truly enjoyed busting my ass trying to somehow get up something like Lost Arrow Chimney . . . or picking out a new route . . . but always feeling good about it. But suddenly it just seems like a drag. Maybe I should have stuck with sports car driving. . . .

■ Perhaps this turned-off feeling will pass; the relaxed atmosphere in the foothill location of *Rock of Ages* is conducive to mending the soul. It's good to be in such fine company . . . Al Steck and Steve Roper sitting at a table playing checkers, mind and vision too dim to cope with the rigors of chess . . . Chuck Pratt whiling away the hours conducting some imaginary symphony orchestra. Truly beautiful to see Earth Mothers, Jan and Beryl, bustling about in their long pioneer gowns, looking after the old fellows. . . .

■ The sun is slowly sinking. Another day is drawing to a close. All the old climbers are putting away their toys and games, soon will be drifting off to their quarters to await the cheery call to dinner. Perhaps some of the more daring will have a small glass of Red Mountain.

■ I remain in my chair a bit longer—I try to probe further back through the years . . . before the Wall of the Early Morning Light . . . but it all seems like "I've seen this movie before" . . . always the good guys vs. bad guys. Maybe I should have played cowboys and Indians; only trouble is, I'd surely have been an Indian!

Royal Robbins and his wife, Liz, on top of El Capitan after his solo ascent of the Muir Wall.

INTERVIEW WITH ROYAL ROBBINS

KEN WILSON, ALLEN STECK, AND GALEN ROWELL

[*Royal Robbins has for more than a decade been the most accomplished rock climber in America. It was natural that* Mountain, *a British magazine with a penchant for personalities, would wish to publish an interview with him. On a trip to England, Robbins was interviewed by Ken Wilson, the editor of* Mountain. *But in between that time and the proposed publication date, Robbins became involved in the most controversial act of his life. He made the second ascent of the Harding-Caldwell route on the Wall of the Morning Light, during which he removed many drilled anchors with the intention of "erasing" the route. □ Wilson's interview, although interesting and revealing, was then hopelessly dated, and he asked Allen Steck and myself to tape a second interview in California, focusing on the issues of the Wall of the Morning Light. The entire interview is reprinted here, as it appeared in* Mountain *18, November 1971.]—G.A.R.*

■ **Wilson:** *Royal, your name is almost synonymous with big wall climbing in Yosemite. How did it all start? What was your first big climb there?*
■ **Robbins:** The Salathé/Steck on Sentinel was my first really big route. I did the second ascent with Jerry Gallwas and Don Wilson. We went prepared for five days and got to the top in two. Even today it seems a fast ascent. We must have been infused with some sort of energy and ability which only comes rarely—it isn't there all the time. In fact it's not really ability, but a combination of elements. I guess it's inspiration. We did some pretty wild things on that climb—things that hardly bear thinking about. At one place we had to make a long traverse. I had to lower my friends who then went across and up to a stance. When it came to my turn as last man I just held the rope—I figured that I could somehow walk across. I had no judgement about such things in those days. I took quite a swing and bounced about 150 ft. across the wall. When I finally stopped I was pretty battered. But we were young and healthy and resilient, and it was O.K.—and we probably saved half an hour just doing that.
■ *You didn't have jumars then, so presumably sack-hauling techniques were pretty rudimentary.*
■ Oh yes—we just took up a thin line and hauled the things up. Looking back, that's another thing that surprises me. We must have been very fit.
■ *So that was a big success. Then what happened? Did you start thinking about new routes?*
■ Well, that was in 1953, and what you have to realize is that climbing wasn't considered very important then. We were doing it totally for the thrill of it, and not because we gained much respect from our peers. There were so few people climbing and there was very little competition.
■ *You mean there was no prestige attached.*

■ Right. If it had been as important then as it is now I would have gone into it more deeply and more immediately, I'm sure. As it was we just climbed off and on for the next few years, and I even went a whole summer without climbing at all. Then, in 1955, we became more focused on climbing—when I say "we", I mean a small group of us, including Jerry Gallwas and Don Wilson, my Sentinel companions. We got interested in the face of Half Dome and here we saw a very great opportunity. It seemed audacious, of course, but you never know . . . This is the sort of attitude that has characterized my climbing since then—the wild thought, the dismissal, the wondering, and finally you really look into it and there is something there after all. Warren Harding was on our first attempt on which we did very badly, climbing very slowly. I spent a whole afternoon just doing one pitch.

■ *Was this the first time you had climbed with Harding?*

■ No, I had climbed with him once at Tahquitz Rock. I remember that well. He had a good reputation at that time. We were doing a short new route; he nailed up one pitch and belayed in a sort of alcove. When I got up there I found he was sitting in slings hanging off two pitons—an angle driven in low down, and a wafer-thin pin driven straight up. Just as I arrived the angle came out, leaving us both hanging from this one little piton. I remember being surprised that I wasn't more afraid . . . I guess it was so 'this or that' that there wasn't much point in being afraid. Anyway, we got another piton in and the moment passed. I remember it very well, though, because that was just the sort of thing that none of our group would have done. We were very careful, and always had quite a lot of pitons at stances. Harding must have been made of different stuff or something.

■ *How have you got on with Harding over the years?*

■ Off and on—in some ways our attitudes are very different.

■ *You're younger than he is. Do you think your feelings stemmed from that, like the aggressiveness you attribute to Peterson in your Tis-sa-ack article?*

■ I'm sure I had at least my share of those unpleasant characteristics, but I don't feel they were operating in this case. I don't feel competitive towards Harding in the climbing sense; I don't think I ever have. It's difficult to know what my feelings really are in a scene like this because there are so many defense mechanisms at work.

■ *How did you get on with Harding on Half Dome?*

■ Pretty well, that time, but Don and Jerry were not as keen on the project as Harding and I. We would have gone on, but they preferred to retreat.

■ *You mean they didn't like big walls?*

■ No, it wasn't that. They had already done a lot in that respect. It was just that things were going so slowly that they thought we didn't have much chance of success—whereas Harding and I would have carried on and made an escape exit to the left if necessary. It seemed possible. Anyway, after we got down I asked Harding if he would be keen to return the following year. We both felt ourselves to be more passionate climbers than the other two, who were, shall we say, more balanced individuals. We were more eager.

■ *But in fact you didn't get together to do the route. Why was that?*

■ I can't remember exactly what happened, but it seems to me that Jerry said he had written to Harding in Alaska and Harding couldn't make it. So we got a young climber named Mike Sherrick to join us. He was brilliant. There are few people who have seemed to me to have as much natural ability as Mike—Chuck Pratt, certainly, but I can't think of any others. As a matter of fact I was really jealous of him because he was one of the few climbers at that time who I felt had more natural ability than I. That was really when I first started being competitive and started pushing myself in a way that I haven't stopped doing since. I suppose I've done this in some ways in order to maintain the pleasant aura of success that made me feel so good in the early days. I liked that so much that I determined to keep it coming, no matter what I had to do to get it.

■ *So you completed the Half Dome route with Gallwas and Sherrick.*

■ Yes, that was a great adventure. We did the route in five days and we suffered a lot from both heat and fear. We were really scared because we hadn't done anything like it before. We took up 1,000 ft. of extra rope, just in case we couldn't get up after the long traverse. We could have used the rope to get down to the ground again, but as it happened it would have been perfectly possible to retreat down our ascent route.

■ *Did you have better equipment by that time?*

■ Jerry had made some copies of John Salathé's fine pitons. Salathé was *the* inventor of hard steel pitons of superlative design, craftsmanship and toughness, and he made them specially for Yosemite because Yosemite demanded a certain type of piton that wasn't available. Others were copying Salathé's pitons too. Jerry made some, and also made the first 1¼" angles. It was the first time that pitons that big had been made in steel. One of the reasons that so many bolts were placed in those days was that we didn't have these big pitons. In fact even they weren't too big; sometimes we placed two bolts because we didn't have 1½" pitons.

■ *Had you improved your hauling methods by then?*

■ No, and we had a very hard time. Two men had to haul all the time, as we had put all the things in one bag. It didn't occur to us to use separate bags. We got so tired of hauling the thing that after the last bivouac we took a chance and tossed it off.

■ *Were you as fit as on your Sentinel climb?*

■ I think so, but this was a tougher climb. It was in 1957, four years after the Sentinel. Considering our success on that, it was quite a long time before we did this new Half Dome route.

■ *It was shortly afterwards that Harding started on the Nose, wasn't it?*

■ Yes, with Mark Powell and various others. At that time Powell was one of the top American climbers. He was a sort of Hermann Buhl figure, with great intensity, drive and determination. He would starve himself to keep his weight down and would make some very bold leads for those days. He and Harding made a really strong team. But then he got injured on an easy climb, which put him out. Harding's other partners came and went, for none of them had the determination that has always marked Harding and made him just the right man for that sort of climb at that time.

■ *You did the Half Dome climb in good style in one push. Did you feel irritated by the way Harding did the Nose?*

■ Well, it would be more apt to say 'the way he was doing it'. At one stage he sent me a card saying: "Why don't you join us? We're this far". I didn't feel too competitive about it; I was happy with Half Dome and I knew that if they did El Cap it would be with different methods, so our position would not be threatened directly. Anyway, I figured that they were adopting the only possible tactics for those days, so I wasn't uptight about it.

■ *But it was generally agreed at that time that a route done in one push was better than one done by siege.*

■ Well that didn't come into it. There was little doubt in our minds that whoever made the first ascent of the Nose had achieved something bigger and better than anything else that had been done. In the early days we dismissed it because we reckoned it would need bolts all the way. But this was just a rationalization of our fear, and Harding was the first to break that fear—partly because he *had* to get up, as Half Dome wasn't there any more and the Nose was the next logical step.

■ *Do you think Valley climbing would have proceeded at such a pace if you and Harding hadn't been there at the same time?*

■ It wouldn't have made much difference. Someone else would have come along. Competition would still have been there. If you're a climber and you want to operate at the top and do good things—important climbing achievements—then you look for the next thing to do. At the time that was El Cap. Obviously the men who did Half Dome were going to feel some kind of reaction against the guys who were working on the next step. And we did—especially because I am more competitive than most. But I wasn't feeling rancorously competitive. I would have liked to have done El Capitan, but I declined to join Harding because it was his scene, and because I didn't want to do it that way, even though I didn't think it could be done any other way.

■ *There was no thought of muscling in?*

■ No.

■ *That hasn't come at all yet, has it?*

■ Yes. I have done it, but I wouldn't do it to Harding because he was my friend. In general, once a climb has been started in the Valley, others leave it alone unless there is some sort of haziness, in terms of rightfulness of property, that people can take advantage of.

■ *Presumably The Wall of the Early Morning Light was like that.*

■ No, I don't think so. Schmitz and Madsen made the first attempt and then gave up. Everybody knew they had. The next party went up and they gave up. But it's just the opposite with this so-called *Aquarian Wall* which Schmitz and Bridwell have been working on and have tried several times.* They are doing it in good style and not using fixed lines and so on. As long as they are there, in any sense, their position will be respected, although it won't necessarily continue that way if they spin it out too long; there might well be someone who'd come along and do it. Few people have the inclination to go in where other people have been working, but it's understood that everyone has the right to. I would if I wanted to, and if they weren't my friends. If it were someone that I didn't care about and was fiercely competitive with—like Ed Cooper, say—then I wouldn't worry.

■ *Was Salathé Wall a direct reaction to the Nose–the next step, so to speak?*

■ It was the logical next step, but I wouldn't describe it as a reaction. Actually, it struck us that the first thing to do was to make the second ascent of the Nose, without fixed lines. But we weren't sure that it was possible.

*Completed in 1971—Ed.

Anyway, we planned for ten days and made it in seven. That was Chuck Pratt, Tom Frost, Joe Fitschen and myself. Two guys climbed while the others prusiked, carrying the supplies. It was really murder. On the second day, when we did 600 ft., the sack haulers were having such a hard time that when Joe and I reached Dolt Tower I descended a few hundred feet to help them out. You must remember that it was all done on prusik knots with conventional shoulder abseils—no brakebars or anything like that. Doing that kind of a wall with those methods nowadays would seem like a hell of a lot of work.

■ *Had your pitons improved by then?*

■ We did it four years after Harding, and we had some bongs by then. How Harding used his stove legs I'll never know. Dick Long was making pins, and Chouinard too. We also had rurps. Chouinard had gone up the first few pitches and chopped some bolts because he found he could use rurps instead.

■ *When did Chouinard appear on the scene?*

■ I can't remember exactly, but it must have been in the late 'fifties. The first thing I heard was that this guy had come out to Stoney Point, where we had done some hard boulder problems. He had done one of mine in better style—and I said 'who is this guy?' So of course everyone then tried to do it in better style.

■ *How can you do a boulder route in better style? Surely you either do it or you don't?*

■ Well you do it with one hand—or even no hands. It didn't really bother me, but I just felt that I would try to do it better. I remember thinking that he had done it on purpose. Chouinard has always been anti-competition on the surface, but I'm not sure that it's that way underneath.

■ *He displays a greater subtlety perhaps.*

■ I think so. My overtly competitive attitude is partly because of my lack of subtlety, and partly because I was part of a group that reacted against the lie of the older generation that there was no competition. We openly accepted it, most of us quite willingly, and in talking about it we figured that it was all right providing one didn't become mean-spirited about it. We thought that it helped advance the standards of climbing. Right now there is a stronger feeling against competition. I know a lot of climbers who feel it has no place in climbing and want to avoid it, but I think most of them are kidding themselves, though there are some exceptions. For the most part it's just fashion.

■ *Presumably Chouinard's was the most important influence in improving the general quality of equipment.*

■ Yes, that's certainly true.

■ *What was his background?*

■ Well, he came to Yosemite from the Tetons for one thing. He lived in California, but he always went to the Tetons to climb. It was only some time after the scene had started in Yosemite that he decided to join it. I'm sure that at first he thought 'that's just rock climbing'. He is a mountaineer first and a rock climber second, but when he finally came he came in a big way. He started making pitons pretty early, just for his own ascents with Tom Frost. At first he made ring angles which were better than those available; the rings were thicker and the design was better. So right at the very beginning he started putting his own touch on his equipment, matching it to the needs of the climb he was doing. He has this amazing ability for getting to the essence of the problem and making the correct piece of equipment. Soon the rurp appeared. It was probably his biggest breakthrough in terms of the influence it has had on climbing. Nothing else he has done has had quite the same effect.

■ *Did it allow harder aid pitches to be done?*

■ Using rurps can make an A4 pitch A2. They allow climbing on a given piece of rock that wouldn't otherwise be climbed except with bolts.

■ *But isn't there a basic insecurity with rurps that automatically makes the climbing more precarious?*

■ No. On a bad pitch you're more likely to get good rurps than anything else. And a good rurp can be quite good. You very rarely hear of them coming out, and they have even held some short falls.

■ *Let's get back to the Nose. You did it with better pitons, but with greater expenditure of effort. Then came the Salathé Wall.*

■ No, you're too soon. We did the Salathé some time after. You mustn't think we were out to grab a new route on El Cap and make a name for ourselves. We weren't interested in that: we were interested in climbing.

■ *What you said previously seems to contradict that.*

■ It's quite possible! Maybe there was a bit of both. Maybe we were just afraid of the Salathé and maybe we felt we had some laurels to rest on. Whatever it was, we spent the next two seasons doing routes in the Tetons and the High Sierra, and other smaller routes in Yosemite. It wasn't until 1963* that we got round to doing the Salathé. I remember when we were in the meadow looking at it and we pieced together a sort of route that looked as if it might go without too many bolts. We had been unenthusiastic about doing another route on El Cap because we didn't want to place 100 bolts. 125 had been placed in the first ascent of the Nose, and a route like that just wasn't worth it to us—it was too much work. But when we saw this line our spirits went up. Imagine a route on El Cap following this round-about line and not using many bolts! We had to get it. We were very, very enthusiastic.

■ *But you thought that pitons would be needed most of the way.*

■ Oh yes.

■ *So the fact that there was a good deal of free climbing was an extra bonus.*

■ Yes. There wasn't all that much though. About 40% of it goes free now, but it was less then.

■ *And the Nose–about 20% now, and 10% then?*

■ I would guess so, unless you're Jim Bridwell or someone, and then it's 40%. We wanted to do the Salathé in as adventurous a way as possible, but we didn't think we could get to the top in one push because of the experience we'd gained on the Nose. We planned to push a route up to Heart Ledge, and then leave fixed ropes to the ground—so we did that in 2½ days and came down. We returned a few days later, prusiked back up the ropes and dropped them behind us. This was making a real adventure of it, because we didn't know whether we could make the top. We were one third of the way up and had placed 13 bolts, and we figured that we might have to place another 20 or 30. Anyway, we just carried on and did the best we could, and we got to the top in six days—without any more bolts. If bolts

*The Salathé Wall was climbed in September 1961—Ed.

had been needed, we might have spent another three days on the climb, and we'd only come prepared for six. We cut it very fine.

■ *It must have been very exciting coming over on to that headwall.*

■ Yes, it was fantastic. We had picked it out from the ground. There's a great overhang with this Vector-like line to the right of where we went, but our line went straight up the most unlikely part—right over the overhangs and up a blank wall cut by one crack. From the ground it looks very dodgy, but somehow we were just led straight to it.

■ *This was on the fifth day?*

■ Yes, but we fixed ropes up half of it, retreated to a bivouac, and returned on the sixth day to complete it. There was one point when I was hanging from two pitons on the wall—Chuck had just cleaned the pitch and the others were all above me on a ledge. They fixed the lines for me, and I got my prusik knots fixed. I was so frightened that I tied a big knot in the end of the rope as well. Finally, I let myself out on the end of the rope for about eight feet; I thought that that would be about right, so I let the rope slip through the piton. But it had been holding me in so much that I swung twenty feet out from the wall—two and a half thousand feet above the ground. I had a good rope and everything, but I was so afraid that I could barely suppress a shout of terror.

■ *It was obviously a tremendous ascent—you must have had as much adventure as you wanted.*

■ We felt really proud that we had judged it right and cut things really fine. We stuck our necks out as far as could reasonably be expected.

■ *The possibility of rescue must have been fairly remote.*

■ Very remote. It might have been possible, but it would have taken several days and there just weren't the ropes around at that time. We figured we would have to be very careful not to get hurt.

■ *What came next?*

■ After the Salathé I did other grade sixes, which were quite hard. On the hardest, Arches Direct, I had three falls on one pitch—one a fifty-footer. Soon after that I went to Europe for the first time.

■ *When did you do North America Wall?*

■ After the Dihedral Wall. It was during the second ascent of that route that I perfected the sack-hauling method that is used now, in order to avoid all that tedious, energetic work. I figured that we would need to improve in technique if we were to do Dihedral in one push. It had taken a total of 38 days and was supposed to be harder than the Nose. We had just begun to use Jumars by then, and we had one pair for the route. So Tom Frost and I had one each. The one who was climbing used a Jumar and a prusik knot, and the hauler had one to make that easier. After that climb we got on to thinking about the N.A. Wall. By that time—after Cooper's team had done the Dihedral and so forth—the competition for big wall routes was becoming more intense.

■ *Did ethics start to develop then?*

■ They already had. We had quite strong views when we did the Salathé.

■ *Then Ed Cooper came along and sieged the Dihedral. Presumably that ruffled a few feathers.*

■ Yes. I was really down on that. He knew how we had done the Salathé, but he was very strange, he didn't communicate. I have never said a word to

Cooper. He just came in and started on this route. We took great offence at this—especially me—because this guy had never done a climb in Yosemite. He carefully avoided that, I thought. He came along to do this big wall and get himself a new route on El Capitan—which we thought should go to those who could do it in better style. Anybody could come along and whittle away at it.

■ *Of course he had done Grand Wall on Squamish Chief.*

■ Well, yes, but stories got down to us that he had avoided some of the cracks because they were dirty, and bolted up blank rock instead. This to us wasn't climbing but something we wanted to avoid. So when, as an outsider, he came down and started applying these techniques to Yosemite, we thought he was being rather presumptuous.

■ *He was the driving force, not Baldwin?*

■ Oh he was the force, no question of that. He was like Harding, but darker and more sombre, without Harding's liveliness. But he did have the same aggression and determination. Glen Denny joined them when they were about halfway up, and he added quite a bit in terms of technical climbing ability, as he had already done a lot in Yosemite. I was very critical then, but I don't feel that way any more. Now I'm a little more mellowed, and it doesn't matter. One has to admit that they did put up a very fine route and they did do a good job in terms of not overplacing bolts. They took 14 days to climb the first 700 ft., which seemed excessive to us. But I have to give them credit for making good use of the time, because they only placed two bolts in getting up there. I thought that was good.

■ *It was very hard presumably.*

■ It was. It's easier now, but I was very respectful when we did the second ascent, because they did such a good job on that part—and all the way, as it turned out.

■ *So your original feelings were irrational.*

■ No, I was right in terms of my own premises, my own frames of reference. Any experienced Yosemite climber could have done that route much faster.

■ *So speed and style were the causes for complaint, rather than equipment and techniques employed?*

■ No, we had to admit once that it wouldn't have been possible without fixed lines. But what galled me most was outsiders coming in and doing what Yosemite climbers were reluctant to do until they could do it in the right way.

■ *Did the same feelings affect you when Ward-Drummond arrived with over-ambitious plans?*

■ No.

■ *But he planned to do North America Wall in an equally presumptuous way.*

■ Yes, but he wasn't going to take anything from me. He hoped to do a second ascent.

■ *But if he had been successful, all the international prestige of the route–the pinnacle of Yosemite climbing–would have been weakened. Surely that would have damaged your credibility and that of Yosemite climbing in general?*

■ I don't think in those terms, and I don't think many American climbers do. The international importance of Yosemite has come as quite a surprise to most of us. We were used to being ignored by the American Alpine Club, for example. It didn't bother us. I was once asked to join, but I didn't see the point of it. We were just interested in climbing in Yosemite. When the article on the Salathé Wall first appeared in the A.A.J., several years after the climb had been done, that was a big thing—we were getting some belated credit for our climbs.

■ *Presumably Chouinard was quite aware of the wider significance of Valley climbing.*

■ Certainly more than any of the rest of us. But we really just weren't interested in publicizing Yosemite. For me, writing an article in the A.A.J. was a little unreal. Since then the explosion of Yosemite in the world scene is much more a thing in the minds of others, particularly the English. You people seem to be taking it more seriously than we ever did, if I may say so. When I first came to England I was made to feel pretty important, and this to me was unreal and surprising, but nice—you know. It's always been a little unreal, so that when you talk of my being knocked off my pedestal it's rather meaningless. The pedestal itself has always been a bit unreal to me.

■ *Let's go back to North America Wall.*

■ By this time things had gone so far that I was getting greedy. I was anxious to get a certain wall before someone else did, and a new route on El Capitan would be that much more to add to one's reputation. So I started thinking more in terms of doing climbs for fame than of doing them just for the fun of it. Glen Denny and I got together and made a reconnaissance. We got about 400 ft. up before I pulled a pin and Denny burnt his hands holding me, so we had to come down. We thought we could go up on another recce, perhaps place any bolts that were needed, and then abseil off, but without leaving any fixed lines. It wouldn't be perfect style: the bolts would help us, and so would the knowledge of the route, but it would still be fairly good style and still be an adventure. So we came back later with Tom Frost, climbed about halfway up the wall, placed about 18 bolts, and arrived at a good ledge which would form a base for work on the upper part of the route. Then we roped off, without leaving any fixed lines. Ultimately, when the time was right, Denny couldn't join us, so Chuck Pratt and Yvon Chouinard came along and we climbed it. The third pitch was really difficult and intimidating. In a way it was much worse repeating it, knowing what it was like. It's a long run of nested, tied-off pitons. The real drawback with not leaving fixed lines was having to do this again.

■ *Were you as apprehensive on this climb as on the Salathé?*

■ More, I think, because of the nature of the upper section. We had to make several pendulums, and it would have been very difficult to retreat. But it was the unknown that scared us most. We looked up and saw what looked like some horrible overhanging cracks that might have to be climbed free. We were very pleased to have Pratt along just in case!

■ *Your ambition seems to have put you somewhat apart from other climbers. How do you feel about that?*

■ Well, it's true. But even though I might have mixed feelings about it, one always goes in the most important direction—most important to oneself, that is. I dislike certain elements in my personality, but I can't honestly say that I would do things any differently.

■ *Do you get much criticism from your contemporaries?*

■ I think my attitudes are resented, but nobody has yet expressed the fact openly—in the way that Frost criticized Whillans in your Annapurna feature, for example. The nearest to that I have had was in letters from Chris Jones and Doug Scott: they came closer than anyone else to saying that I am over-ambitious and selfish.

■ *Let's move on to the Alps now. When did you have your first season?*

■ In 1962. I met up with Gary Hemming on Chamonix, and we did a new route on the Dru. I had climbed with Hemming very early on, and our paths had criss-crossed through the years. I was very sorry when he died.

■ *It's said that he was a man of great emotional extremes.*

■ That's true. Part of the reason why he went in the direction of drugs, spiritualism and mysticism, which he did to some extent, was that he had such turbulent emotions and wanted to control them. He wanted an answer, a way of dampening the suffering he was going through most of the time. Climbing was a way of doing this. He thought—obviously we all do—that if he did a certain climb things were going to be better. Anyway, he had all the ideas. He knew our particular rock skills. The line on the Dru was just right for the time—a major new line on a big wall. And it was hard. If I had been John Harlin it would have been splashed all over Europe. But we didn't view things that way. Obviously the competition was there among climbers, but the outer world was something we were trying to get away from, not become noticed by.

■ *You appear to be contradicting yourself again.*

■ I'd be foolish to try to resolve these contradictions. I'm just trying to give an honest impression. I'm not in the least bit interested in being noticed by the general public, newspapers, television and the like. But having the respect of climbers is something else. In the old days I felt I wanted the respect of my peers. Some people, like John Harlin for example, thrived on all types of publicity. He just wanted as much as possible coming from any direction. I'm not quite that way.

■ *Incidentally, when did Harlin appear on the scene?*

■ I met him in Philadelphia, at the American Alpine Club meeting that was so laudatory towards Yosemite. I spoke on Yosemite, and in the evening he spoke on his ascent of the Eigerwand. There was an atmosphere of euphoria at that meeting. The successes on the Eiger, in Yosemite and on Everest gave one the feeling that one was witnessing a renaissance in American climbing. Harlin was an extraordinary person. He took me in completely, just as he did many others. It was his subtlety and the strength of his personality. I thought he was motivated by good ideals and wanted to do good things, generous things. Later I changed my opinion about that and decided he was someone else entirely.

■ *Do you think he used the climbers around him?*

■ I think he used anybody he could. That's the main thing I objected to. I remember when we were in Chamonix once, without transport, and he wanted to go to the Calanque. There were two English climbers there, and he said: "I'll go over and talk to these guys—I can get them to do anything I want." He put it in such a way that it rather shocked me, because I didn't believe in using people. It sounded as if he would indeed use those guys by the sheer force of his personality. That was the first thing that turned me off a bit. Later I saw more and more of this aspect of him, and I realized that if he hadn't respected me for being a better rock climber he would have had contempt for me too. He had contempt for anyone who was weaker than he was.

■ *Did he enjoy the company of people who were better than him?*

■ My impression was that he used them so that he could get as good as they were. If he ever did, they could be dismissed.

■ *What was his relationship with Kor?*

■ Much the same, in my opinion. Kor liked him a lot, just as guys like Dougal Haston did; Haston had the greatest respect for him. I don't think Harlin thought too highly of Kor though. Kor could certainly nail better, but no doubt Harlin thought that if he worked on it, he could nail well too. He probably thought highly of Haston, though, because Haston was better at things than he was. Harlin asked me to go on the Eiger Direct with him, but I declined because I'm not an expedition man and I didn't want to be involved with getting someone else to the top of a mountain. Also I didn't really understand that type of climbing and would have been too much out of my element.

■ *You did a new route on the Dru with Harlin. Whose idea was that?*

■ His. I had looked at it earlier and thought it a nice line, but we have many routes like that in the States. I didn't really see the point in coming all the way to Europe for that. So I wasn't too ambitious, but Harlin persuaded me. When I got to the bottom I was keener, as it was a good line on good rock. If you've been doing it for years, climbing a steep granite wall for three days just isn't adventure any more—you know you can do it.

■ *There was the weather factor, though.*

■ Yes, we did have that risk, and I thought that here I was not completely within my own element. Actually, after Harlin got injured, I felt we really were playing the climbing game for keeps. Much of the terror of the big walls of Yosemite is illusory, but here was a situation where death was really looking at us. Oddly enough, I wasn't afraid, and that was odd because generally I am in those circumstances.

■ *What about Harlin's climbing ability?*

■ Well, he was the greatest American alpinist of his day. Harlin had a genius for getting publicity, though, and he let a lot of misleading things develop. The idea that he cut his teeth on El Capitan—or that he was a Yosemite climber at all—is all nonsense. When we brought Yosemite techniques to the Alps, or in particular, when Gary Hemming did, Harlin took all the credit for it. But he had nothing to do with it, except that he jumped on the bandwagon. That sort of thing was what made us object to Harlin: he was so good, and yet he needed to do that.

■ *Bonington has said that Harlin was responsible for pointing American climbers to Alpine possibilities. The South Face of the Fou was cited.*

■ Well he didn't point Hemming and me at the Dru. Harlin saw what we'd done and went on from there. But other people had seen these routes too. And anyway, when it comes down to it, I did most of the leading on the second Dru climb, and Frost and Hemming did the leading on the Fou. It wasn't that Harlin wasn't capable of leading, but just that he took all the credit for the climbing when actually his greater achievement was in public relations.

193

■ *And motivation?*

■ He had a lot—I don't doubt that—but somehow it seemed out of balance.

■ *You haven't been back to the Alps since then?*

■ Not to climb. I would like to do the Walker Spur some day, and possibly the Eiger, but it's getting to be such a problem fighting all the people on them that they don't attract me so much any more. But don't get me wrong—I have no illusions about the difficulty of the Eiger. I didn't agree with my friend Dornan's deprecating remarks in his review of the Harlin book in *Ascent*.

■ *Since your visit to the Alps you seem to have been looking for more serious tests in your visits to Alaska and your solo climbs in Yosemite.*

■ That's true.

■ *Is this because the Alps made you think that Yosemite was intrinsically safe?*

■ No. I realized that long before I went to the Alps.

■ *But you didn't solo Muir Wall before. Was that inspired by Bonatti's route on the Dru?*

■ Not directly, though of course Bonatti's superb feat stands as a great example to us all. Bonatti, I think, is in the great tradition. He should be emulated. His achievements are neither technological nor technical tricks, but are primarily achievements of the human spirit, and that goes deepest. For me, at that time, Muir was just the next obvious step. In order to feel that I had achieved something comparable to our original Half Dome route, I had to solo it. It might have been even harder, but the main point was that for me it was in the same category, with the same blend and balance of tension, as the Half Dome climb.

■ *What about Alaska?*

■ We just went to make some first ascents, and to get some alpine climbing, which was something new for me. I wanted to get away from pure

rock. When I went to the Alps I wasted my time doing rock climbs when I could have been learning alpinism. Nevertheless, when I go back to Alaska I would like to do a big wall—the sort of climbing that I know, but in much more formidable conditions.

■ *What about Cerro Torre?*

■ I would love to climb that!

■ *Do you agree with Chouinard that climbing big walls in alpine conditions is the logical extension of present developments?*

■ Certainly. Quite apart from being interested in making a reputation and some money, my primary reason for climbing is still the personal thing it gives me. If I didn't have those other things I would still be doing mainly what I am doing. I'm still going in the direction I started off in . . . trying to find some sort of peace of mind in doing the ultimate climb that will make everything else all right. To me, it used to be N.A. Wall, or something like that, but some time ago I realized that the ultimate challenge in mountaineering is the one that makes the greatest demands on the maximum number of human qualities. The Eiger has always been the epitome of this. Look, to do these big new routes in Yosemite, you needed ability and competence, certainly, and also things like a spirit of adventure, strength, a certain agility, an intelligent knowledge of rock climbing, and a bit of endurance. On the Eiger you need all these things and many more. Therefore it's a higher level of achievement. I want to do a climb that takes the ultimate—and still succeed.

■ *Although most of the climbs you've done have been free of objective danger, you did have it on the Dru.*

■ We had a storm on the way down, and I felt that we were in a very exposed situation. If we had been caught on the wall it would have been very serious, and I've heard some fearful stories from friends of mine that have been caught there in bad weather.

■ *So you feel that this is an experience that you've missed.*

■ Yes. Even climbing the Muir Wall solo—probably my biggest rock-climbing adventure and potentially the most dangerous—was still completely controllable. It all turned really on my own skills. But in bad weather, when you put self-control up against all kinds of things that you haven't been through before—well, that's a much stiffer game, and a more lifelike one. I think that the more you can approximate the rigours of climbing to the rigours of life, the more complete a game it is. The Eiger is the best example I can think of. It's a very dangerous mountain, and if things turn bad your chances of coming out of it O.K. are immeasurably greater if you're a Buhl, a Rebuffat or a Whillans, than if you're one of many other mountaineers that have gotten on the thing. In other words, even though the technical difficulties and the objective dangers are very great, it still turns mostly on your personal qualities. It's such a demand on these qualities that it's hideously frightening in a way—a real measure of a man.

The preceding conversation took place in London, in October 1970. Soon after Robbins had returned to the States, Warren Harding and Dean Caldwell made their highly controversial ascent of the Wall of the Early Morning Light. The American climbing world became divided into two schools of thought: one condemned the number of bolts used and the large amount of publicity that the climb attracted in the popular press, while the other maintained that these were minor flaws compared to the climbers' magnificent achievement in making a 27-day climb. Many people held both points of view. Two months later, Robbins and Don Lauria repeated the route in six days. In the process they removed a number of the offending bolts from the earlier pitches, yet, curiously, did not continue to do so on the later ones. In some ways this second ascent was even more controversial than the first, for it raised questions of interference, ethics, and a whole range of issues that face climbers, not only in California, but throughout the world. Clearly, our interview was now out of date, so we arranged for some further discussion to take place in the States. Allen Steck (Editor of Ascent) *and Galen Rowell acted as our representatives, and the following conversation took place at Steck's house in Berkeley, California. Readers should note that although the official guidebook title of the route in question is* The Wall of the Early Morning Light, *it is referred to throughout the ensuing interview as* The Dawn Wall.

■ **Rowell:** What was the original idea behind your Dawn Wall ascent? Did you set out to eliminate or change the existing route, or were you just planning a normal second ascent?

■ **Robbins:** Good question. It's hard to sort that out. In fact, it's almost impossible. I have always wanted to climb every route on El Capitan, but for weeks before we did this one I was wondering what the climb meant for Yosemite, what sort of creation it was, and what should be done about it if it was really as bad as it seemed. I considered several answers, and I'm not sure that I picked the right one. But anyway, we went ahead with a climb that was really based on a desire to remove what we thought was a blot on the Yosemite landscape.

■ **Rowell:** Was the decision to chop the bolts motivated purely by the fact that there were so many on the route, or were you influenced by the almost shameful amount of publicity the climb received?

■ **Robbins:** No, we were influenced solely by the way the route was done. If we had thought it was a valid route, and no criticisms had been levelled at it, we would have accepted it as the future of Yosemite climbing. But we thought it wasn't valid and, having come to that conclusion, we decided that we should do something about it. It was *that* decision that we acted on. The publicity had nothing to do with it; we may have been repelled by this, but none of our actions were based on it.

■ **Steck:** Did Lauria share your views?

■ **Robbins:** Well, that was funny, because I was under the impression that he was all for erasing the route. When I called him and asked him to come and do the second ascent, he was keen. Then, when I said that I understood he was interested in stripping the bolts, he said he didn't mind, but would go along with anything I wanted to do. Well that really put it on my shoulders, because I'd expected him to be keen to do it. Lauria shouldn't be depicted as a climbing fanatic: he's a fine climber, he's easy-going, he has a big, broad smile, and he enjoys life and climbing. He isn't the sort of person who would go out in a petty way to put someone else down. He certainly didn't do that here, although he did feel something of the way I felt about the values involved.

■ **Steck:** Why did you go out so soon to erase the route? Wouldn't it have been better to have waited a little?

■ **Robbins:** Well, I remember going to see Schmitz and Bridwell to talk the thing over. They were all for erasing the route, especially Bridwell, and they were seriously considering doing it themselves. I was keen on doing the second ascent and seeing what the route was like, so I suggested that I should do this and leave the third ascent and the problem of erasing the route to them. But they said that if I did this, it would give the route currency, and they wouldn't subsequently take the drastic step of erasing it. In other words, to repeat the route once, without erasing it, would be a form of approval. So that way they put me in a spot. In the end I didn't say what I was going to do, but I did say that if I climbed the route I would do *something* about it.

■ **Rowell:** By removing the drilled anchors after using them for aid, you deliberately violated the first-ascent principle stated in your own book. In doing this, were you acting rather like a policeman who goes through a red light to catch a speeder?

■ **Robbins:** I didn't really violate it. This was an exception to the rule, because it was an exceptional situation. What I said in the book was that we shouldn't change routes or improve them: we should leave them in their first-ascent state. Here, our idea was to remove the route entirely.

■ **Rowell:** Weren't you worried about people misunderstanding your motives—believing that you were making a personal attack against Harding, for example?

■ **Robbins:** That was one of the most difficult parts of the whole thing. It was pointed out that I put my reputation at stake by deciding to do this in the first place. But my concept of what should be done did not include a personal attack on Harding: as I said in *Summit,* I admire Harding because he is a great exponent of individualism, which I think is one of the most important features of climbing. It's one of the things I came into climbing *for.* Harding and I differ in our methods, and sometimes he does things that I feel are harmful to the spirit of Yosemite climbing. But that's a question of philosophy, and has nothing to do with Harding as a person.

■ **Steck:** The interesting thing about this whole controversy is that nobody will understand that, because everyone believes that it *was* a personal attack.

■ **Robbins:** Maybe, but it's a misconception. I wasn't attacking Harding, I was defending a point of view about Yosemite climbing. The difficulty was to decide what to do. I spent a lot of time thinking about that. I had already said something in my book about technique—that one shouldn't remove bolts from established routes. Clearly, people were going to say that this was inconsistent with what I was going to do on Dawn Wall, and they would damn me for it. I had to put up with that. I also had to put up with the fact that many people would say that my Tis-sa-ack route on Half Dome was simply a scaled-down version of Dawn Wall, and again I would be condemned for being self-contradictory. Obviously, I was going to have a lot of explaining to do. And even then many would think that I had done the wrong thing, either because they couldn't—or because they wouldn't—understand my reasoning. I was, as Ken Wilson said, "laying my reputation on the line". I had enjoyed a number of good things from this reputation—it does make life a little easier, so long as you don't have too much fame—and I had to consider that I might be giving all that up. The safest thing would have been to do nothing—level a bit of criticism perhaps, but no more. But after thinking about it I decided to go ahead with it anyway.

■ **Rowell:** If you had to do it all over again, would you do the climb in the same way—taking out the same number of anchors, that is?

■ **Robbins:** That's a really good question, Galen. It's so obvious I hadn't really thought about it. No, I wouldn't do the same thing again; I'd—boy, I don't know what I'd do. I guess I'd either climb the route without interfering with it, or not climb it at all.

■ **Rowell:** Do you have any basic objection to bat-hooks or rivets? And if so, why?

■ **Robbins:** I object to anything that makes bolting easy, because by making it easy you make it more likely. The good thing about bolting in the past was that you had to work to do it. But if placing a bolt or a bat-hook becomes easier than placing a piton—and Caldwell himself has admitted that it was easier to place rivets than A3 pitons on the climb—then automatically there will be a tendency to reduce the level of climbing: as soon as people get in difficulty they will take the easy way out and place a rivet instead of working at the problem.

■ **Steck:** Don't you have to work to place a rivet?

■ **Robbins:** Not very hard. It's about one-third harder to place an A3 pin than a rivet, and two-thirds harder to place a bolt.

■ **Steck:** What exactly is a rivet?

■ **Rowell:** What Caldwell used were very thin swaged metal cable loops hung over lumps of metal he had hammered into the rock. He would drill a shallow hole—perhaps ⅜ inch deep—and then hammer in the rivet until the entire thing swelled. The cable loop is just draped over the head of the rivet while it is being hammered. If you hammer it properly, you can take the loop off afterwards and use it again.

■ **Robbins:** Anything like that is semi-permanent. Bat-hooks are, too, because eventually the holes get filled with bolts. Rivets are the same. Placing a bolt should be a conscious act of transgression; and that should minimize the number used. If you put a bolt in, it's there for eternity. That's a statement. But if you move that statement towards more and more indefinable limits—well, doubtless we'll have suction pads soon. All of this goes to make up the difference between what I consider the essential spirit of climbing and just 'getting up'. Making bolting easier, with bat-hooks, rivets, pneumatic bolt guns and the like, leads to what are merely technological victories over routes.

■ **Steck:** Surely the Salathé piton was a means to technological victory in its time, wasn't it?

■ **Robbins:** Placing it still required skill, but it requires little or no skill to place a bolt.

■ **Rowell:** There I would disagree. Harding once said that the only way he got up Mt. Watkins was by taking over the drilling, because Chouinard and Pratt were incapable of doing it fast enough. Placing A1 and A2 pins is certainly easier than drilling bolt holes, I think.

■ **Robbins:** It's easier, but there's nothing to that either. The main point is that pitons don't violate the rock.

198

■ **Rowell:** Is that really true? A while ago I heard a couple of climbers discussing this point, and they were of the opinion that only nuts and bolts should be carried on new routes: they felt that new climbs should be done as far as possible on nuts and, when that was impossible, bolts should be placed. That way, they said, they would have a permanent anchor point and avoid all the piton scarring of repeated placements. At first I was horrified with the idea, but after thinking about it I see that it has some merit.

■ **Robbins:** That sounds good, but it doesn't work out in practice. I would certainly like to see more chocks and even bolts used to eliminate pitons, but people won't do that, of course. There are lots of climbs that could be improved like that. I'm not totally against bolts: I've used enough of them myself. I'm just against anything that encourages *pure technology*. I deplore the idle drilling of holes in rock just to get up, and the way this is justified as part of the climb. Placing bolts should be a conscious *outrage* that you unwillingly accept because it is necessary. I think it's important to stress that bolting is raping: you want to avoid it wherever you can.

■ **Rowell:** But would it be rape in the situation I have just described?

■ **Robbins:** I don't know. I'm not saying my way is the answer in every case; different situations demand different answers.

■ **Steck:** Let's get back to the climb. How did you come to ask Lauria to climb it with you?

■ **Robbins:** TM Herbert had told me that Don was keen, so I gave him a ring. He's about my age—sort of older generation—and he was fun to do it with. Once he gets on a climb he'll stay there and keep working on it: he doesn't psyche out. He's a very hard man really. Since the climb, Don has really been put on the hot seat down south in LA; as he wasn't so passionate about the thing as I was, he doesn't quite know what to say. His position is that it was my scene.

■ **Steck:** Well, you probably have to accept that.

■ **Robbins:** Sure, I'm willing to accept responsibility for the whole thing.

■ **Rowell:** There was a lot of sympathy for that route down south. At a party at Chouinard's, a few weeks after the first ascent, I happened to ask if anyone wanted to go and climb it with me the following spring. Almost everyone in the room was keen to do the second ascent.

■ **Robbins:** To leave it up—not to erase it.

■ **Rowell:** That wasn't discussed there, but it was in the newspapers. In the *San Francisco Chronicle* I read: "a young, moustachioed climber said, 'we will do it next spring and cut all the bolts' ". So others had certainly thought of the same thing.

■ **Robbins:** Yes, I knew that. But I felt that although it was being talked about by a lot of people it wouldn't actually get done, because it would be such a grossly outrageous act. I felt that if it was going to be done it would have to be me who did it.

■ **Steck:** At what point on the climb did you change your mind and decide not to chop any more bolts?

■ **Robbins:** We started up with the intention of eradicating the entire route, because we thought it invalid. Harding and Caldwell had strong enough views about their action to spend twenty-seven days on the rock proving their route had merit, and they got a lot of currency for that, because the climb was hailed as a triumph here and there. But we felt that

regardless of the human qualities involved—the toughness and the
doggedness they showed—the climb did more harm than good to Yosemite.

■ **Rowell:** You seem to be returning to the publicity angle again.

■ **Robbins:** I'm not saying that we didn't react to the publicity—just that it
wasn't the motivating factor in our actions.

■ **Rowell:** But it did have something to do with it.

■ **Robbins:** Not with what we did, no. It was their action on the rock that
counted. Here was a route with 330 bolts. It had been forced up what we felt
to be a very unnatural line, sandwiched between other routes, merely to get
another route on El Capitan and bring credit to the people who climbed it.
We felt that this could be done anywhere; instead of 330 bolts, the next
route might involve 600 bolts, or even double that. We thought it was an
outrage and that if a distinction between what is acceptable and what is not
acceptable had to be made, then this was the time to make it. They had put
their beliefs on the line by doing the route, and we put ours on the line by
removing it—by saying just as strongly that we disagreed with them. There
was only one way to answer their action, and that was by an even stronger
reaction. So we started climbing, using and then chopping the bolts. Then
Don went the wrong way and got strung out on a really hard crack system.
When he came down, he said: "I wonder if we're doing the right thing". It
was this hard climbing that made him reflect. In other words, he felt that if
the route had first-rate climbing, regardless of bolts, it was questionable
whether our action was right. Well, the route *does* have first rate climbing,
and when we reached the point of our first bivouac, about four pitches up,
I realized this, and also realized that there was going to be more of it. That
night I lay awake in my hammock thinking about it, and I finally decided that
I no longer felt right about destroying the route. My inner feelings weren't
going along with it, and I would be crossing myself if I kept on doing it. So
the right thing at that point seemed to be to stop the bolt chopping and just
concentrate on climbing the route. At that stage, too, I thought about what
the hell people were going to think. We'd started out doing something and
now, through weakness or whatever, we'd changed our minds. Everyone
was going to feel that we'd started something we didn't have the strength to
continue. So I was faced with this existential problem which I could see
quite clearly: should I act for the sake of consistency, which would certainly
bring me harsh criticism, or should I stop something I now felt was
wrong—and by doing so look like a fool? I decided I had to stop, because if
my actions were going to be motivated solely by consideration of what
people would think, I was finished anyway. So I talked to Don in the
morning, and that's what we did.

■ **Steck:** And you found very challenging climbing?

■ **Robbins:** We found some of the hardest nailing I have ever done, until
we got near the top, and there we found a few ridiculous things like rivets
placed next to good nailing cracks.

■ **Steck:** But imagine what state they were in after being on the wall for so
long.

■ **Robbins:** Right. For the most part the climbing was of high calibre, and
I didn't expect that. There was one good lead after another; both Caldwell
and Harding must have been climbing at a really inspired level. And that, of
course, complicated the whole thing enormously—how could one continue
to judge it so simply? Essentially it means that Harding won. The main point

now is that the thing should be *explained,* not that somebody should be made to appear right or wrong. It's a contest between attitudes and ways of doing things. We acted on theory, and it seems clear now that we would have been better not doing it that way. But it looked right at the time, and the iron was hot, so we took the risk that we might turn out to be doing the wrong thing. But everyone makes mistakes. I'm happy to admit that this was one.

■ **Rowell:** My impression of this controversy when it first came up was that there was a tremendous lack of communication between you and Harding, and between climbers and the public. Are you sure that your decisions weren't warped by the tremendous amount of publicity generated by the climb, by the fact that it was hailed as the greatest climb ever done and so on?

■ **Robbins:** There have been a lot of ascents of El Cap—like the Kroger/Davis Heart Direct, for example—which no climber could question. Nobody could have anything but admiration for that. It was done in supremely fine style; and, to take a more recent example, so was Peter Haan's solo ascent of the Salathé Wall. He hadn't even done a grade 5 or a grade 6 route before, yet he used no new bolts and no new techniques; the whole climb turned on a question of the human spirit. It was marvelous: no climber could find any way of disputing that. I just think that, despite all the fine things that characterize the Dawn Wall ascent, the fact that they had to do it in that way left it open to criticism. It was a half-and-half thing: half admirable and half unfortunately damnable, because it led towards the rape of Yosemite. My point of view was that El Capitan had been raped, and that this would encourage other climbers to perform further heartless rapes, instead of taking the rock with love. This was what I objected to, and this was the threat I have been trying to explain here.

■ **Rowell:** I played devil's advocate for about four hours the other day in an argument between TM Herbert and Harding. I can't recall their exact words, but I can remember that the discussion got absolutely nowhere because it was as if there was a glass plate between them. Warren kept on saying things like: "I am an individual. . . I don't give a damn what you think, I'll do what I want to do because I want to do it and you can't stop me . . . Climbing is not a sport that's institutionalized . . . it's not organized and nobody can tell me what to do".

■ **Robbins:** Trouble is, he *does* give a damn.

■ **Rowell:** I agree with you there. Then Herbert's view of it was all tied up with tradition, what's been done before, what we have to look forward to in the future, and how we as a group of climbers have to look at our sport, and so on. They had two completely different sets of values. One of them couldn't convince the other because they weren't talking about the same values.

■ **Robbins:** That's one of the things I admire about climbing: there are all these ways of self-expression. You can appreciate all the different climbers for the different contributions they make. But the guys who work in the higher levels of climbing are doing their things particularly well. Harding is doing his thing well, but the trouble is that his 'thing'—his great genius—involves a change in something that affects everybody else directly. His great quality is that fantastic doggedness—but the only way you can express doggedness in Yosemite is to find a route that takes a lot of bolting, because there aren't any 6,000 ft. routes. If there were, Harding would be doing the finest climbs around. He could stay up there and fight—just with pitons. But he has to create 6,000 and 9,000 ft. routes by finding rock that's so blank that climbing it is just like doing a 9,000 ft. route—and we say that's O.K. for Harding, but it's going to lead to bad things for Yosemite. Of course I may be totally wrong to get so up-tight about this. Allen here takes a really good view, a relaxed view: "things are what they are" . . . but when I ask him about this, he doesn't have a real answer.

■ **Steck:** One of the things one has to consider is that every generation that comes along wants to be original and have new avenues to explore. So there are people who are keen for new lines, but find that there isn't much scope.

■ **Robbins:** The irony there is that good lines are being done—Davis' and Kroger's route, for example. Yet it is Harding, who has been around for quite a long time, who is doing the things we are critical of. I think there are three avenues of progress. The first is to put up ever more questionable routes on blanker and blanker rock; the second is to accept the challenge of doing climbs in finer style; and the third is to go elsewhere to find new routes. If it's accepted that anything anywhere is valid, then anything is going to be put up anywhere. It degrades the rock—no question about that—and it may lead to a point where there are 100 routes on El Capitan, instead of 20, which would be about right. We don't want endless routes everywhere, because that, as I say, degrades the rock. But, more important, it degrades the meaning of the routes that already exist. So I feel that while one can accept routes like Leaning Tower and the South Face of Half Dome—single routes up blank virgin faces—the searching on El Cap was searching too far, and that made the difference.

■ Rowell: That brings up a point that Ken Wilson made: wasn't the Tis-sa-ack route on Half Dome just a scaled-down version of Dawn Wall?

■ **Robbins:** Well, there are several things I could point out here, such as the fact that we used proportionally less bolts, and the fact that any route that uses a bolt could be called a scaled-down version of Dawn Wall—but that isn't important. What *is* important is that I felt it was valid. The route on Half Dome was going to be done because it was a natural line—a broad area of rock that was bound to have a route sooner or later. I knew it would be done and I also knew that there were enough connecting cracks, so that we wouldn't need an excessive number of bolts. In the event we placed thirty more than we expected, and that was twenty more than we actually took on the climb.

■ **Rowell:** How many drilled anchors altogether?

■ **Robbins:** One hundred and ten. But the determination of a route's validity according to the number of bolts placed has to be totally arbitrary. There is no logical line to be drawn—or if there is I haven't heard of it. If you agree with the proposition that one bolt on an El Cap route is O.K., but 1,000 are not, then somewhere between you have to draw a line. And that line is totally arbitrary, based solely on your sense of proportion. My sense of proportion tells me that Tis-sa-ack was all right, but Dawn Wall was going too far. Here was a big new climb on El Cap that violated my feeling of what is right in Yosemite climbing. And a lot of other people thought the same. But the point is that if somebody feels as strongly about Tis-sa-ack as we did about Dawn Wall, then they are certainly welcome to erase that. And they would be right to do so. Jones mentioned this in his letter to *Mountain*—and I say: O.K., if he feels that way then he ought to do it, even if it means starting from the top (which incidentally would be rather difficult). I would not object at all. I would rather give up a few routes and retain good values in the Valley.

- **Rowell:** But what does taking bolts out of a route really do?
- **Robbins:** It eliminates the route.
- **Rowell:** But it doesn't take away the first ascent.
- **Robbins:** No, it certainly doesn't.
- **Rowell:** So it's really just a symbolic act to show people that somebody objected?
- **Robbins:** Yes, it's symbolic, but it's also going to make a very real impression.
- **Rowell:** And what does it do to the person who made the first ascent?
- **Robbins:** Well, a friend of mine told me that while we were on Dawn Wall Harding was really worried about us, because he knew that with 150 ft. ropes we could find it difficult—there are some really long leads. My friend said: "There was Harding feeling sorry for you while you were up there chopping his route all to hell." So I told him: "Don't you worry about Harding; he can take care of himself. He can give out as good as anyone else, and he doesn't need pity."
- **Steck:** Do you think this controversy has much relevance to climbers in Britain?
- **Robbins:** Some of the guys over there are almost obsessed with matters of ethics and pure lines and so on. And I think it's a good thing. From my own point of view, I love Yosemite: it means a lot to me and I've been climbing there for twenty years. I've grown up with certain values and I believe in certain things, and I hate to see something I love raped. But I got all my values about climbing from Great Britain. After all, Britain produced Geoffrey Winthrop Young, who said it's not getting to the top that counts, but how you do it—and it strikes me that the lads over there wouldn't put up with a bolt ladder right next to Cenotaph Corner. It just wouldn't be allowed to remain there.
- **Rowell:** But that's a totally different situation. There's no tradition of bolt-placing on that type of cliff, whereas the first route on El Capitan had bolts in it.
- **Robbins:** That's not the point. The fact is that they would feel it was an outrage, and they'd act on that feeling—and that justifies *my* feeling and *my* action.
- **Rowell:** Well, it doesn't quite work like that. I think lots of people will go on talking about being anti-bolt, but they'll still keep packing a bolt kit when they go off on a climb.
- **Steck:** Oh! I don't know—there may be a new trend coming in Yosemite climbing—removing routes.
- **Rowell:** We figured this, and you started the trend, Robbins.
- **Robbins:** Oh, come on!
- **Rowell:** No, it's right. We figured that every route on El Cap had offended somebody, somehow, and that the end result would be that every route would be chopped and we would end up back at square one with no routes at all!

GLOSSARY

Aid: artificial climbing in which mechanical aids such as **pitons, bolts** and ropes are used for body support. The same equipment may be used for **free climbing,** but for safety only, not as a means of upward climbing or resting.

Aid slings: stirrups usually made from inch-wide nylon tape. They are used as rope ladders and attached to anchors by **carabiners.**

Angle piton: a piton made for cracks ½ inch wide and larger. A cross section resembles the long sides of the letter "A".

Arête: a steep and narrow ridge on a mountain or rock wall.

Bat hook: a device used for **direct aid** in shallow drilled holes, invented by Warren Harding to save time on long blank cliffs where **bolts** would otherwise be necessary.

Belay: as a verb this word means to feed the rope to the leader from a secure position in such a manner that it could be held in case of a fall. As a noun **belay** means the entire safety system on which the leader depends. A "bombproof belay" is one in which both the position of the belayer and the anchors holding him are ideally secure.

Bivouac: in general and in military use, this word means simply a night spent out in the open, but in climbing it denotes a night spent during the course of a climb.

Bolt: see **expansion bolt**

Buttress: an outside corner or projection of a mountain or cliff somewhat wider than an **arête.**

Cairn: a pile of rocks left as a marker on a summit or as a means of indicating a route, similar to a blaze on a tree.

Carabiner: a metal snap-link about three inches long which resembles a giant safety pin and is capable of holding more than a ton. Carabiners are used for attaching the rope to anchors in rock or snow.

Chimney: a long crack large enough for a person to enter, often climbed by cross-pressure between knees, back, feet and hands. When a chimney is narrow it is called a squeeze chimney, and if it is narrower yet, a **jam crack.**

Chocks: see **nuts**

Class one, two, three, four, five and six: parts of a rating system for the difficulty of climbs. **Classes one through four** do not require belaying through anchors and are not often mentioned in reference to Yosemite. **Class five** is **free climbing** using a **belay** and **pitons, nuts, runners** or **bolts** for protection. **Class six** is aid climbing. The difficulty of free climbing is expressed in decimals of **class five,** 5.1 being easy and 5.9 being very difficult. As standards have progressed, climbers have found it necessary to add 5.10 and 5.11, but **class six** is rated by the symbols A1 to A5. Not only are fewer categories needed for **aid** climbing, but to use decimals of the number six would be confusing since **class five** climbs are often more difficult than **class six.**

Cliffhanger: see **skyhook**

Dihedral: an inside corner where two rock planes intersect. Sometimes called an **open book** because of the resemblance to a partly opened book. Cracks usually occur at the intersection, and dihedrals are an important part of route-finding on the smooth walls of Yosemite.

Direct aid: see **aid** and **class six**

Exfoliated: a term describing rock that is peeling like the surface of an onion. The photograph of Half Dome on page 3 shows a perfect example.

Expansion bolt: a device designed for anchoring in concrete which climbers use in a drilled hole when cracks are not available for **pitons** or **nuts.**

Face climbing: utilizing foot and hand holds on an open rock face as opposed to **jamming, chimneying** or using **aid.**

Fixed rope: a rope left in place after a pitch is climbed so that climbers can ascend or descend at will. To **fix** a pitch means to climb a distance and leave a rope. Most expedition climbing uses fixed ropes to facilitate load carrying and fast retreat over difficult terrain, but Yosemite climbing in the past decade has rejected the use of fixed ropes to a large degree.

Glossary

Free climbing: climbing in which upward progress is entirely unsupported by mechanical aids. A rope and hardware may be used for safety only. The opposite of **aid,** or artificial climbing. (see **class five**)

Friction or **friction climbing: face climbing** on **slabs** where foot and handholds are slanted and the climber uses friction rather than defined holds.

Jam crack: a crack running vertically which is climbed by jamming part of the body into the fissure. A thin jam crack may be only large enough for a climber's fingers, whereas a wide jam may admit a shoulder and a leg. A jam crack large enough to admit the climber's whole body is called a **chimney.**

Jumars: a brand name of mechanical ascenders used to climb fixed ropes and often to follow behind the leader on long climbs. Jumars grip the rope when pulled down, but slide freely upward so that with foot slings a climber can ascend a 150-foot rope in a matter of minutes. (see **Prusik**)

Lieback (sometimes written as **layback**): crack climbing using counterpressure between hands and feet. See photo on page 85.

Nailing: aid climbing using many **pitons** in a row.

Nuts: artificial chockstones usually made of aluminum alloy and threaded with nylon cord. They are fitted into constrictions in cracks, and can be used most of the time in place of **pitons**, which scar the rock if removed and replaced frequently. Nuts are relatively new to Yosemite but have already replaced **pitons** on most of the popular one-day climbs. On these routes a few **bolts** or **pitons** may be left in place and the climber can do the route without carrying a hammer, since nuts can be lifted out of their placements.

Open book: see **dihedral**

Pitch: a unit measure of climbing, meaning a distance covered in one rope length. Some pitches may be nearly as long as the rope (150-165 feet). Others may be as short as 50 feet if they are difficult and there is no stopping place above. Obviously the term is very flexible, but a three-pitch climb is usually that for all parties, whereas an El Capitan route might be 28 pitches for one party and 30 pitches for another that chose different belay points.

Pitons: a metal wedge driven into a natural crack in the rock with a hole or a ring at one end for attaching a **carabiner.** Pitons come in all sizes from Rurps the size of postage stamps that fit fingernail-thick cracks to bong-bongs that fit cracks wider than a man's foot.

Primus: a brand name of a simple, light, gasoline-fueled stove. Often used, as *Frigidaire* is for refrigerators, to mean any small gasoline stove regardless of brand.

Prusik: a technique for climbing a rope. This word was originally confined to the use of Prusik knots but is now used for rope climbing with **jumar** ascenders. The knot, invented by Karl Prusik many years ago, will slide freely when unweighted but grips tightly to the main rope when weight is applied to it.

Rappel: a technique for descending a rope in which friction of the rope across the body or through **carabiners** is used to control the rate of descent. A doubled rope is used so that it can be retrieved by pulling one end, requiring only the leaving of **piton** or sling anchors at wide distances on the descent of a climb.

Rope traverse: see **tension traverse**

Runners: loops of nylon rope or tape that have many purposes. They can be used in place of **pitons** or **nuts** on climbs having upward-pointing projections; they can be used to lengthen the anchor on **pitons** or **nuts** to make the rope run more easily; they are like baling wire to the mechanic—often used to temporarily attach almost anything to anything else.

Scree: a collection of small, loose rocks, usually below a cliff. **Talus** is a collection of larger loose rocks that normally don't slide when you walk on them.

Skyhook: a small hook used for **aid** on tiny ledges when cracks are not available for **nuts** or **pitons.**

Slab: a smooth section of a cliff which is steep but somewhat less than vertical.

Sling seat (also called **belay** seat): a piece of strong, light cloth with sewn straps that can be attached to an anchor point for long hours of sitting on a blank wall without a ledge.

Talus: see **scree**

205

Tension traverse: direct-aid climbing in which a climber crosses a traverse with the aid of a tight rope from behind, using hands and feet on the rock to counterbalance the side pull of the rope.

PHOTO CREDITS

This book was typeset in 11 point Optima, with chapter titles in
  Weiss Series I, and printed on 70 pound coated Tahoe gloss.
Typesetters: Johnson Printing Plates, San Francisco